Building Your Own Compiler
with
C++

Jim Holmes

Bethel College, MN

Prentice Hall
Englewood Cliffs, NJ 07632

Library of Congress Cataloging-in-Publication Data

Holmes, Jim
    Building your own compiler with C++ / Jim Holmes.
        p.   cm.
    Includes bibliographical references and index.
    ISBN 0-13-182106-7
    1. Compilers (Computer programs) 2. Object-oriented programming
(Computer science) 3. C++ (Computer program language)   I. Title.
QA76.76.C65H63 1995
005.4'53--dc20
                                                          94-36754
                                                              CIP

Acquisitions Editor: Bill Zobrist
Production Editor: Bayani Mendoza de Leon
Copy Editor: Brenda Melissaratos
Cover Designer: Wendy Alling Judy
Buyer: Lori Bulwin
Editorial Assistant: Phyllis Morgan

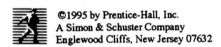 ©1995 by Prentice-Hall, Inc.
A Simon & Schuster Company
Englewood Cliffs, New Jersey 07632

The author and publisher of this book have used their best efforts in preparing this book. These efforts include the
development, research, and testing of the theories and programs to determine their effectiveness. The author and
publisher make no warranty of any kind, expressed or implied, with regard to these programs or the documentation
contained in this book. The author and publisher shall not be liable in any event for incidental or consequential damages
in connection with, or arising out of, the furnishing, performance, or use of these programs.

SUN and SPARCstation are registered trademarks of SUN Microsystems, Inc.
UNIX is a registered trademark of AT&T

Printed in the United States of America

10 9 8 7 6 5 4 3 2

ISBN 0-13-182106-7

Prentice-Hall International (UK) Limited, London
Prentice-Hall of Australia Pty. Limited, Sydney
Prentice-Hall Canada Inc., Toronto
Prentice-Hall Hispanoamericana, S.A., Mexico
Prentice-Hall of India Private Limited, New Delhi
Prentice-Hall of Japan, Inc., Tokyo
Simon & Schuster Asia Pte. Ltd., Singapore
Editora Prentice-Hall do Brasil, Ltda., Rio de Janeiro

Contents

Preface   **vii**

1 Project   **1**
  1.1 Project Description   1
  1.2 Project Requirements   1
  1.3 Suggested Activities   2

2 Objects and Classes   **3**
  2.1 Encapsulation   3
  2.2 Hierarchy   5
  2.3 Late Binding   7
  2.4 Suggested Activities   8

3 Analysis and Design   **13**
  3.1 System Analysis   13
  3.2 System Design   15
  3.3 Summary   23
  3.4 Suggested Activities   24

4 Main()   **27**
  4.1 C++ Main Function   27
  4.2 C++ Concepts   27
  4.3 Makefile   29
  4.4 Summary   30
  4.5 Suggested Activities   30

5 System Control   **31**

5.1   Controller Module   31

5.2   Module Makefile   38

5.3   Summary   38

5.4   Suggested Activities   38

6   The Scanner/Parser Module   **41**

6.1   The Encapsulator: ScanparseCls   41

6.2   The Scanner: **yylex()**   45

6.3   The Parser: **yyparse()**   53

6.4   Module Makefile   59

6.5   Summary   59

6.6   Suggested Activities   60

7   Symbol Table Module   **65**

7.1   Symbol Table Module Header   65

7.2   ScopeCls   65

7.3   SymtabEntryCls   66

7.4   SymtabCls   67

7.5   Module Makefile   72

7.6   Summary   73

7.7   Suggested Activities   73

8   Parse Tree Nodes   **75**

8.1   An Example   75

8.2   Description of Module   81

8.3   PTreeNodeCls: The Base Class   81

8.4   NumLiteralCls   84

8.5   IdentCls   84

8.6   ExprCls   85

8.7   StatementCls   86

8.8   LstSeqBldrCls   87

8.9   StatementSeqCls   88

8.10 BlockCls   89

8.11 ProgramCls   90

8.12 PTreeCls   91

8.13 Summary   91

8.14 Suggested Activities   92

9 Implementing Parse Tree Behavior   **95**
  9.1   PTreeNodeCls: Header   95
  9.2   PTreeNodeCls: The Base Class   95
  9.3   NumLiteralCls   96
  9.4   IdentCls   97
  9.5   ExprCls   99
  9.6   StatementCls   101
  9.7   LstSeqBldrCls   102
  9.8   StatementSeqCls   102
  9.9   BlockCls   103
  9.10 ProgramCls   103
  9.11 PTreeCls   104
  9.12 Module Makefile   104
  9.13 Suggested Activities   104

10 Interpreter Module   **107**
  10.1 Statements   107
  10.2 Statement Sequences   108
  10.3 Higher Level Classes   109
  10.4 Makefile   109
  10.5 Suggested Activities   110

11 Emitter Module   **111**
  11.1 Chapter Overview   111
  11.2 A Simple Example   111
  11.3 Emitting Symbol Table Entries   114
  11.4 Expressions   115
  11.5 StatementCls   116
  11.6 Higher Level Classes   118
  11.7 Producing the Executable   119
  11.8 Makefile   120
  11.9 Suggested Activities   120

A Program Code   **123**
  A.1   Main   123
  A.2   Controller   123
  A.3   Scanner-Parser   126
  A.4   Symbol Table   131

A.5 Parse Tree Nodes   135

B Answers to Activities   **147**
   B.1   Chapter 1 Activities   147
   B.2   Chapter 2 Activities   147
   B.3   Chapter 3 Activities   155
   B.4   Chapter 4 Activities   161
   B.5   Chapter 5 Activities   164
   B.6   Chapter 6 Activities   168
   B.7   Chapter 7 Activities   178
   B.8   Chapter 8 Activities   182
   B.9   Chapter 9 Activities   183
   B.10 Chapter 10 Activities   192
   B.11 Chapter 11 Activities   193

Bibliography   **195**

Index   **197**

Preface

Understanding does not usually come by merely reading through a text nor even religiously working the exercises at the end of each chapter. For most of us, real learning requires extensive involvement. That means time spent in picky details as well as in general ideas. In computer science we can experience such involvement by actually trying to build a hardware or software representation of the topic at hand. That's what this book is all about. We're going to *build* a compiler.

This book was originally designed to be used as a project illustrating the ideas in *Object-Oriented Compiler Construction* [5]. The close parallel between the chapters of the two books serves as a guide for coordinating their reading. The various compiler components presented in both texts occur in roughly the same order and use essentially the same ideas. If this describes your purposes, you are strongly encouraged to use the specific text examples as only a starting point for you own work, adding more advanced features as time and interest permit.

More recently this text has been used in a stand-alone mode, serving as a modest introduction to C++ and providing an example of an actual compiler that is sufficiently simple that it can be programmed with a reasonably small amount of effort on several different programming platforms. People using the text in this manner are often computer professionals having a particular interest in the construction of compilers. Even though every effort has been made to produce a self-contained text for such readers, most theoretical details are necessarily omitted and can be obtained from other references cited in the bibliography.

A SUN SPARCstation[1] running UNIX[2] is used for the example in this text, though the code and ideas in this workbook have been ported fairly easily to PCs and other workstations. Chapter 1 contains information about the equipment and software required for the project. A brief introduction to object-oriented programming is found in Chapter 2. Chapters 3–11 contain the code and construction details related to the example compiler program.

A complete source listing of the example compiler has been placed (with some apprehension) in Appendix A. Line numbers have been added to this code as well

---

[1] SUN and SPARCstation are registered trademarks of SUN Microsystems, Inc.

[2] UNIX is a registered trademark of AT&T.

as to all other listings within the text for reference purposes only and are of course not part of the actual source code. There is always a temptation to merely enter program code directly[3] rather than to work through the construction process. But we understand a system better when we build it ourselves. Appendix A should therefore be viewed more as context and less as an exact pattern for your work.

---

[3] Actually, the entire system, complete with makefiles, is available via anonymous ftp from *ftp.bethel.edu*. It is in the compressed tar file *epc.tar.Z* in the *pub/epc* directory. Additional information about *internet* and *ftp* can be obtained from Krol's excellent text [7, pages 59–90].

Chapter 1

Project

1.1 Project Description

**To build an interpreter and compiler for a
very small subset of Pascal using C++ as the
implementation language.**

The project described in this text, while not large by today's software standards,
does provide an opportunity for extended work on a specific problem. By the time
you have built a compiler that only slightly extends the example described in the
text, you may have several thousand lines of C++ code.

1.2 Project Requirements

We all have experienced the wide gulf between our best ideas or designs and the
final actualization of the product. One factor that often limits the quality of the
final product is the availability of appropriate tools. The tools we use to build
software are primarily aids to our thinking and to our mental precision rather than
the reduction of physical effort. But even here, the size and character of the final
system will depend in a number of tangible ways on the development tools that are
available.

1.2.1 Hardware

Most of us have access to computer hardware that is more than sufficient for the
project in this text. In fact, the project can be completed on a very minimal system,
by simply scaling back on project size or by building particular components in
ways that demand less of the platform. If possible, you should probably have
sufficient hardware to support the execution of a nontrivial editor, an object-
oriented compiling system such as C++, and several tools that are used to build
compiler components. To keep development time down to a reasonable level, this
might mean having at least an Intel-386 PC or a workstation, a minimum of 4
megabytes of memory, and at least 100 megabytes of additional storage on a disk.

1

1.2.2   Software

Operating system.   Begin to collect information about your operating system. Does it support a directory structure? Do you have an assembler? Collect any documentation you can find on the required form of assembly language programs. Do you have several editors? Is there a stream editor? If not, are there ways you can modify files in some automated way?

Object-oriented environment.   It certainly is possible to use the methods in this text without having a compiler or development system for an object-oriented language. However, quality systems are becoming widely available for a number of different platforms and at prices that are usually quite affordable. The object-oriented code in this text is C++. The examples will be of more direct help to you if you build your own compiler using that language. However, there are many other fine object-oriented systems that you might use if you do not use C++.

Compiler component generators.   Depending on how closely your project matches that of the text, you may need utilities that generate compiler scanners and parsers. The normal UNIX *lex* and *yacc* are fine. If they are not available, try to locate similar shareware utilities, such as the corresponding Gnu utilities *flex* and *bison*.

Project development tools.   You will need some system for maintaining your project as it is being developed. When working on a programming project, we can often lose track of which files need to be recompiled after a change is made to some part of the system. It is also very difficult to recall or even correctly enter a particular command that is required to process various pieces of the system.

This text uses the UNIX *make* utility, that provides a simple mechanism for producing up-to-date versions of programs out of a number of different modules. Some C++ systems, especially those designed for PC environments, have this capability built into the compiling system.

1.3   Suggested Activities

Locate system documentation on the use of the system's assembler, editor, and existing compiler tools. Then evaluate your development platform by completing the following table.

Component	Presently Available	Planning on Obtaining
CPU and speed		
Amount of memory		
Additional disk space		
Existence of assembler		
Editor		
Automated editing		
Tools (e.g., *lex*, *yacc*)		
Project development tools		

Chapter 2

Objects and Classes

2.1 Encapsulation

Objects encapsulate data and have behavior. In C++, objects are **typed** or classified by describing a **class**. An object is often called an **instance** of the class. In this text we tend to think of class description as a two-step process consisting of a **class definition** and a **class implementation**.

Class definition. The usual C++ syntax for defining a class consists of a **class head**, composed of the **keyword class** and a **tag name**, and the **class body**, enclosed by braces and terminated with a semicolon. This information is usually placed in a **header** file, such as *sample.h*.[1]

```
 sample.h

1       class SampleCls {
2         public:
3             SampleCls();
4             void        print();
5             int         behavior1();
6         private:
7             int         data_member;
8             int         behavior2();
9       };
```

Data declared public are accessible to the functions of any class. Public functions can similarly be called by any function. Access to private data or functions is restricted to member functions of this class.

In the example above, the first function specified in the public section is called a class **constructor**. It is executed when a *SampleCls* object is created. The second function *print* is just used to display information about the particular object. The keyword **void** just indicates that the function returns no value. The third function is just a public class behavior.

---

[1] Throughout the text, the name of the source file is displayed in the small box. Line numbers are included only for discussion and are not a part of the actual code.

The private members of *SampleCls* consist of one integer data member and an integer-valued function or behavior.

Class implementation.   Class implementation is usually placed in a separate file, such as *sample.C*.

```
sample.C

 1 #include <stream.h>
 2 #include "sample.h"
 3
 4 main() {
 5     SampleCls *ps = new SampleCls;
 6     ps -> behavior1();
 7 }
 8
 9 SampleCls :: SampleCls () {
10     cout << "SampleCls()" << endl;
11     this -> behavior2();
12 }
13
14 int SampleCls :: behavior1 () {
15     cout << "SampleCls::behavior1()" << endl;
16     return 1;
17 }
18
19 int SampleCls :: behavior2 () {
20     cout << "SampleCls::behavior2()" << endl;
21     return 2;
22 }
```

The first `#include` just imports the normal C++ input/output classes so that `cout` and `endl` are available. The second imports the *SampleCls* definition.

The function *main()* is required of all C++ programs. After system initialization, control is passed to this function. In this case we are simply creating an instance of *SampleCls* (an object) and storing its address in the pointer *ps*. Since *behavior1()* is public, *main()* can invoke it.

The *SampleCls* constructor prints out an identifying message and calls its own *behavior2()* member function. At runtime, the pointer `this` contains the address of the object using the particular member function. There are some applications, for example, certain window applications, where `this` is an essential programming tool (Lippman [8, page 194]). The use of `this` in the example compiler is more a matter of aiding the reader of the code. Often a particular member function will call a number of functions associated with many different objects. Here, its use simply serves to emphasize that the particular function being called is a member function for `this` object. Note also that the constructor does not return a value and that it has access to its own private data or behaviors.

2.2 Hierarchy

When we start to build a system using object-oriented methods, we are usually first confronted with arranging the various pieces of the system into groups or classes. System components are placed together if they perform similar tasks or need access to related information, or communicate extensively with each other.

One effective way to collect things into classes is to put items in the same class if they have identical or related behavior. If the objects have exactly the same behavior, the classification can proceed by defining a base class encapsulating that common behavior. However, if some of the objects have similar but nonidentical behavior, then they can be arranged into classes that are derived from the base class. Any behavior that is common to all the objects can be placed in the base class. Behavior that is distinctive to an object can be placed in the definition of the derived class. *Similar* behaviors can be handled by defining a default or **virtual** base class behavior and then redefining it for each derived class as may be necessary.

In the following code, there are two public member behaviors. The first one is shared, i.e., is utilized by all objects, either of *BaseCls* or *DerivedCls*.

```
hierarch.h

 1 class BaseCls {
 2     public:
 3         BaseCls();
 4         int     common_behavior();
 5         virtual int similar_behavior();
 6     private:
 7         int     common_data;
 8 };
 9
10 class DerivedCls : public BaseCls {
11     public:
12         DerivedCls();
13         int     unique_behavior();
14         int     similar_behavior();
15     private:
16         int     unique_data;
17 };
```

The second member behavior, since it has been declared **virtual**, will be utilized by all *BaseCls* objects, as well as those of a class derived from *BaseCls* unless the function is redefined as illustrated in *DerivedCls*.

The code on page 6 illustrates what we call the **class implementation** or **implementation module** as N. Wirth would call it in his later languages. Note, especially in *main()*, that a base and derived object are created and that various combinations of the class member functions are called.

hierarch.C

```
 1 #include <stream.h>
 2 #include "hierarch.h"
 3
 4 main() {
 5     BaseCls *pb    = new BaseCls;
 6     DerivedCls *pd = new DerivedCls;
 7     cout << endl;
 8
 9     cout << "common behavior: base " << pb->common_behavior() << endl;
10     cout << "common behavior: drvd " << pd->common_behavior() << endl;
11     cout << endl;
12
13     cout << "unique behavior:  " << pd -> unique_behavior() << endl;;
14     cout << endl;
15
16     cout << "similar behavior, base: " << pb->similar_behavior() << endl;
17     cout << "similar behavior, drvd: " << pd->similar_behavior() << endl;
18 }
19
20 BaseCls :: BaseCls() {
21     cout << "BaseCls()" << endl;;
22 }
23
24 int BaseCls :: common_behavior() {
25     cout << "BaseCls::common_behavior()" ;
26     return 0;
27 }
28
29 int BaseCls :: similar_behavior() {
30     cout << "BaseCls::similar_behavior()" ;
31     return 1;
32 }
33
34 DerivedCls :: DerivedCls() {
35     cout << "DerivedCls()" << endl;
36 }
37
38 int DerivedCls :: unique_behavior() {
39     cout << "DerivedCls::unique_behavior()" ;
40     return 123;
41 }
42
43 int DerivedCls :: similar_behavior() {
44     cout << "DerivedCls::similar_behavior()" ;
45     return 2;
46 }
```

Executing this code produces the following output.

```
BaseCls()
BaseCls()
DerivedCls()

common behavior: base BaseCls::common_behavior()0
common behavior: drvd BaseCls::common_behavior()0

unique behavior:  DerivedCls::unique_behavior()123

similar behavior, base: BaseCls::similar_behavior()1
similar behavior, drvd: DerivedCls::similar_behavior()2
```

There are a number of items that are of particular interest to our compiler construction activities.

- The instantiation of a *BaseCls* object invokes the corresponding constructor.

- The instantiation of a *DerivedCls* object *first* invokes the constructor of the base class and then the constructor of the derived class.

- *Common_behavior()* is available to both base and derived objects.

- *Unique_behavior()* is available only for a derived object.

- *Similar_behavior()* will be the base behavior for base objects and derived behavior for those *DerivedCls* objects that have redefined the base behavior.

2.3 Late Binding

Let's modify main() as follows.

```
 hierarch.C

  4 main() {
  5     BaseCls *pb     = new BaseCls;
  6     DerivedCls *pd = new DerivedCls;
  7     cout << pb -> similar_behavior() << endl;
  8     pb = pd;
  9     cout << pb -> similar_behavior() << endl;
 10 }
```

In this case, we first create a *BaseCls* object and print out its *similar_behavior()*. We then create a *DerivedCls* object and store its address in the old base class variable.

The new version of *main()* now outputs the following information.

```
BaseCls()
BaseCls()
DerivedCls()
BaseCls::similar_behavior()1
DerivedCls::similar_behavior()2
```

Notice that the *same command* now prints out the *similar_behavior()* of the object *assigned* to the variable. Late binding! This is probably the most important feature of object-oriented programming that we use in our construction of the compiler.

2.4   Suggested Activities

1. (Experiment with C++)

    (a) Write a C++ program that outputs the following message.

    Hello world!

    (b) Write a C++ function to read characters from stdin and produce a tally of:

        i. The number of white spaces.

        ii. The number of non-white-space characters.

    (c) Write a C++ main program that calls the function in the above exercise. Test it on a number of different kinds of input.

    (d) (A useful class for possible future application)

    Write a C++ definition and implementation for *StringCls*, a class that abstracts the notion of strings. Be sure to include members for data storage, a constructor that converts the usual (char*) C++ string to *StringCls* and some means for a *StringCls* object to output itself.

2. (Classes: Encapsulation)

    Let's imagine that we have to work with two C functions *function1()* and *function2()*, which communicate via a global variable *glbl* as illustrated in the following code.

```
 1 #include <iostream.h>
 2
 3 int glbl = 0;
 4
 5 void function1() {
 6     cout << ++glbl << endl;;
 7 }
 8
 9 void function2() {
10     cout << --glbl << endl;
11 }
12
13 main() {
14     function1();
15     function2();
16 }
```

It is not too difficult to think of situations where we would like to avoid
using such globals, but would not want to or even be able to rewrite the two
functions (Chapter 6). However, it is possible to use the notion of a class to
encapsulate the global and the functions.

(a) (Definition of C++ classes) Define a class *EncapsCls* that has a public
    constructor an the following three private members.

  - An integer variable *glbl*.
  - A void function *function1()*.
  - A void function *function2()*.

   Place your definition the class definition file *encaps.h*.

(b) (Implementation of C++ classes) Place the following information in the
    corresponding implementation file *encaps.C*.

  - Preprocessor **include** commands for *stream* and *encaps.h*.
  - *EncapsCls* constructor implementation. Have this function contain
    an initialization of *glbl* and then the two calls to the functions pre-
    viously contained in *main()*.
  - *EncapsCls :: function1()* implementation.
  - *EncapsCls :: function2()* implementation.

(c) (Main module) Write an appropriate *main()* that creates an *EncapsCls*
    object. Place this in a separate main module, *main.C*.

(d) (Separate compilation)

   i. Only compile *main()*, suppressing the linking by using the *-c* option
      as follows.

      ```
      CC -c main.C
      ```

ii. Compile the encapulator module, again with a command something like the following.

```
CC -c encaps.C
```

iii. Link the object files *main.o* and *encaps.o*.

```
CC  main.o encaps.o
```

iv. Test the execution of the system.

3. (Classes: Derivation) One possible extension of the example compiler is to add error detection and reporting capabilities. It turns out that the detection can be easily accomplished by slightly modifying the classes already implemented in Chapter 9. We therefore only need to design and implement objects that can be used to report the errors to the user.

   (a) Analysis.

   - Make a list of the various kinds of messages you will want to send to the user. Also be sure to consider warning messages.
   - Are there any common features or behaviors of the system for the various messages?
   - What are the features or behaviors of the system that are unique to each kind of message?

   (b) Design.

   - Define *MessageCls*, a class encapsulating any data or behavior members that are common to all the various errors and warnings. Be sure to include some form of printing behavior.
   - Define the various kinds of error and warning classes by deriving them from *MessageCls*. Consider making the *MessageCls* print behavior virtual and then redefining it for the derived classes as may be necessary. What happens if you do not make the base class print behavior a virtual function but include print behaviors for the derived classes?

   (c) Implementation.

   - Implement the constructor(s) and behaviors for *MessageCls*. Carefully test the various member functions.
   - Implement the various error and warning classes. Perhaps it would be best to implement and test one derived class at a time. Be especially careful to note the order of execution of the derived and the base constructors. Also verify that the print behaviors of the derived classes is exactly what you have in mind. In particular, take whatever steps are necessary to ensure that the base class print behavior is not being used if it should not be.

4. (Classes: Late Binding)

   For sake of discussion, let's say that *Derived1Cls* and *Derived2Cls* are two of
   the error or warning classes derived in Activity 2.3, above, that have print
   behaviors sufficiently different that they can be distinguished. Make a test
   program that does the following.

   (a) Contains a variable *base_ptr* of *MessageCls* * type.

   (b) Creates *Derived1Cls* and *Derived2Cls* objects in free store (i.e., on the
       heap).

   (c) Places a pointer to the *Derived1Cls* object in *base_ptr* and then executes
       the objects print behavior using something like the following command.

   $$base\_ptr-> print()$$

   (d) Also place a pointer to the *Derived2Cls* object in *base_ptr* and executes
       its print behavior by issuing exactly the same command.

Chapter 3

Analysis and Design

Actually, object-oriented analysis/design is often a dynamic and repetitive process that is not easily illustrated in print. This chapter contains a first pass at analyzing the example compiler at a high level, followed by a very modest design effort. Subsequent object-oriented design activities contained in the remaining chapters often raise questions that require modifying the analysis specified in this chapter. The inclusion of these later analysis documents would certainly be appropriate in those later chapters but has been omitted in the interest of saving space.

3.1 System Analysis

3.1.1 Traditional Software Engineering

What should the example compiler do?

- How much of the Pascal language should the system be able to compile?

- Should the system be able to deal with errors in the source file?

- How should the compiler interface with the user? What command invokes the compiler? What options should be available?

How much of the Pascal language?   Let's agree that the example compiler should be able to handle the subset of Pascal represented by the following program.

```
Representative Pascal Program

1    program simple;
2    begin
3        j := 3;
4        i := j;
5        writeln(i)
6    end.
```

Of course, this means that the scanner must be able to recognize keywords like `program`, `begin`, and `end`; it should also be able to recognize the special symbols like the semi-colon and left and right parentheses. Since there are no type or variable declarations in the sample program, all variables and expressions must be of some common type (say, `integer`) and variables will be declared when first encountered in the source program.

The compiler is to function both as an interpreter and a compiler. Suppose that we agree that when compiling it should only produce executable code for a particular SUN SPARCStation platform.

How to handle errors?   Detecting and reporting programmer errors is quite involved. Also, since this compiler is to be used primarily by an expert (you!), we can safely assume that the source programs will usually be error free.

We will therefore agree to not include facilities for error checking in the initial construction phase. We may, however, want to add such features in later versions.

What kind of user interface?   Compilers often interface with users by accepting a set of options and an input file name, usually on the same line as the command invoking the compiler. If we call the compiler *epc* for *Example Pascal Compiler*, a command like

$$epc\ -l\ prog.p$$

should therefore produce a source listing and result in the corresponding source program being interpreted, rather than compiled. Perhaps the command

$$epc\ -e\ prog.p$$

should produce an executable file *a.out* but no source listing.

3.1.2   Object-Oriented Analysis

Now let's focus on the task of discovering the classes and the objects used in the example compiler.

A good place to start, especially for a small projects, has been described by Abbott [1] who suggests that we begin by writing an English description of the problem and then underlining the nouns and verbs. The nouns are good candidates for objects and the verbs are possible behaviors.

> Our compiler translates a tiny subset of Pascal into SPARC assembly language. It also will interpret such source programs by executing each instruction.

> Traditionally, compilers have consisted of several components. The source code is converted into a string of tokens by a scanner. This token stream is then converted into a parse tree by the parser. A parse tree consists of nodes, each of which represents the various instructions and expressions occurring in the source.

> Normally, the parse tree is converted into assembly language by a code generator. In our case we will provide the nodes of the tree with the

ability to <u>generate</u> their own code. Similarly an interpreter normally traverses the tree. Again, we will each node with the behavior to <u>execute</u> each instruction and <u>evaluate</u> each expression. code.

Obviously not every noun in the above description will necessarily be an important object in our compiler. Likewise, all the verbs are not automatically behaviors of the objects. We can narrow the search a bit by using the definition of object given in Booch [3].

> An object has state, exhibits some well-defined behavior and has a unique identify.

In our compiler description, above, those nouns satisfying (at least some of)the state-requirement seem to be the following.

- Scanner.

- Parser.

- Various Parse Tree Nodes.

We could (and should) be more precise about the various kinds of Parse tree nodes. Indeed at this early stage of analysis we can probably only think of two kinds of instructions.

- Assignment.

- Output.

Similarly there are only two kinds of expressions.

- Numeric literals

- Identifiers representing variables.

It therefore looks like we will need to construct classes that abstract the attributes and behaviors of a scanner, a parser, and various parse tree nodes, some related to source program instructions and others related to expressions.

3.2 System Design

How shall we develop the system? Shelf software components, like shelf electronics components, must be able to be conveniently packaged into highly independent modules. When systems have a large number of essentially independent subsystems, even object-oriented methodologies recommend the use of prepackaged classes. But when the major parts of a system are significantly dependent upon one another, the shelf analogy is totally inadequate.

3.2.1   Some Lessons from Biology

Biological systems, particularly the higher forms, exhibit this kind of interdependence complexity. Almost every major component of an organism depends on nearly every other major member for its own existence, as well its functionality. It is instructive to note that in nature, the production of such systems is a process of *development* or *growth*. Granted, even at the beginning, entire system analysis and design are coded into its complex DNA, but each new system is grown from a single cell each time.

Vertebrates are complex organisms that start their existence as a one-celled zygote. From the time the zygote divides and its nucleus reproduces itself, cells are quickly being produced and collected into special groups destined to become the major "components" of the organism.

The embryonic stage is the first major phase of development. During this time, the organism assembles the cells into a ball-like **blastula** or **morula**. This blastula soon begins to change. There are local changes: Cells actually migrate on the surface of the blastula. There are global changes: The overall shape of the blastula changes. This process of shape-changing and even moving various cells around on the blastula is clearly a way of grouping various cells into primitive presystem clusters. Cells begin to assume properties and perform tasks specifically related to their position in the overall system and the nature of their neighbors.

Several observations are relevant.

- The first major effort of the developing organism seems to be the rapid construction of an embryo, which is a *functioning* system having most of its major subsystems in place.

- These subsystems are often primitive, but each one contributes to the performance of the developing organism. The particular shape or form of the subsystem often is dictated by the role that a similar system plays in less complex but related organisms.

- These subsystems almost always consist of immature structures that will become the mature components of the organism. Subsystems can mature in one of two major ways.

  - Most frequently an immature system gradually changes (increases in size and functionality) into its mature form.

  - Sometimes a small part of the immature system actually matures into the final version of the subsystem, while the rest gradually declines in size or in some cases is even destroyed (programmed cell death).

It is important to note that at each stage the *future development* of the organism depends in large measure on the extent to which the present stage of the developing embryo *successfully works as a system*.

The analogies for object-oriented design and implementation are numerous. Software "embryos" are not feasibility prototypes, nor are they throw-away code. Object-oriented embryonic code actually *matures* into the final system.

It is also helpful to note that these early systems are not just the first step in the traditional top-down development process. In no sense does the code represent a high-level routine making calls to subprogram stubs. The components of the system may be in various stages of development, but all are functioning as subsystems and contributing to neighboring subsystems if not to the entire system.

Three specific implementation guidelines are derived from the biological model.

1. The implementor must specify at the earliest possible stage a collection of essential subsystems. A subsystem is *essential* if other subsystems depend on the existence of the subsystem.

2. The implementor must have a well-planned *implementation schedule* for the various subsystems. The system must continue to function as the various systems are added. This may require the *simultaneous* development of a number of systems.

3. Implementation of new systems and enhancements of existing systems must directly depend upon the previous configuration of the system. New systems are added precisely at the point that they can meaningfully interact with existing systems.

The implementation work also provides an early verification of the integrity of the overall system design. Classes can be carefully defined; time analysis and function analysis all precisely performed. However, the ultimate test is still whether all those objects work together as a system.

3.2.2 Strategy for System Development

List of essential systems. The software guidelines above indicate that the first phases of development should include only essential subsystems. Compiler construction is a well-developed area of computer science. The components found in an object-oriented compiler (Figure 3.1) are essentially the same as those found in a traditionally constructed compiler: scanner, parser, symbol tables. The scanner translates the source code into a stream of tokens or integers describing the original program lexemes. The parser checks the tokens for correct syntax and then builds a parse tree, along with appropriate symbol tables. The objects out of which the tree is constructed have the ability to either interpret the original source program or to emit assembly language code corresponding to the source program. We will also add a controller to the list of components. Its major role is to coordinate the construction of the higher level objects. It will first check user-selected options and then create an object encapsulating the scanning and parsing functions.

The system can therefore be viewed as consisting of the following modules.

1. *main* . Contains only the (C++) required function *main()*

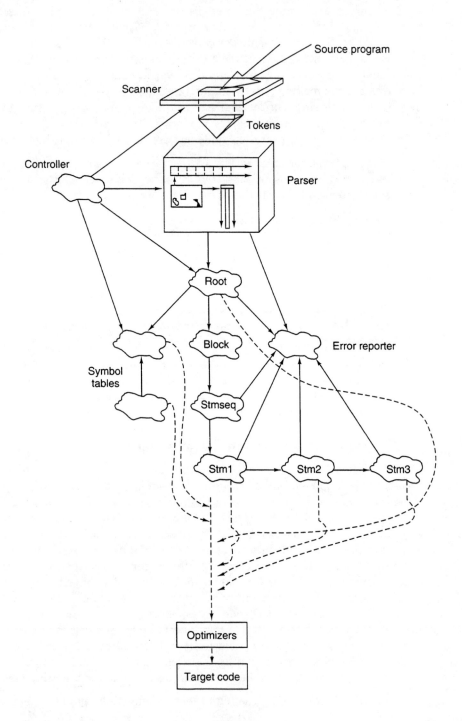

Figure 3.1. Compiler Structure

2. *ctrl* . Contains the definition and implementation of *ControllerCls*, a collection of objects responsible for system control

3. *scanparse* . Contains the standard scanner and the parser procedures. It also contains the definition and implementation of *ScanParseCls* that encapsulates the scanner and parser

4. *symtab* . Contains the definition and implementation code for the symbol table entry classes, as well as the definition and implementation details for the symbol table class

5. *p_tree* . Contains the definition and (much of) the implementation for the parse tree nodes used by the parser. It is the most important module.

6. *interp* . Contains the *execute()* implementation details enabling the parse tree to interpret the original source code. This is really a continuation of the *p_tree* module.

7. *emit* Contains the *emit()* implementation details enabling the parse tree to output target code

Obviously, as you build your own compiler, you might profitably arrange the modules in a manner different from our arrangement that involves twelve files located in seven different directories, as illustrated in Figure 3.2. Often the files in one module depend[1] on the contents of a number of definition files from other modules. This dependence is indicated in Figure 3.2 by arrows pointing *to* the included file.

Development plan. Since each subsystem relates to at least one other system, it is a bit of a challenge to find which pieces to implement first or which part of a particular system to try to have ready to interact with other parts of the system. Figure 3.3 is an attempt to establish developmental milestones in terms of files or groups of files. Each grouping signifies what is called a *compilation stage* in which the entire embryo must consist of nontrivial objects, must compile, and must run acceptably (at least as an interpreter) on test data that match the system's particular state of development at that compilation stage.

Although displaying each module at each of these compilation stages might be instructive, the extensive amount of C++ code in various phases of development would probably prove to be uninspiring reading and might not provide as many insights as you would want. The following chapters therefore contain completed versions of the various modules of the system. It will probably be more useful for you to lightly read the completed code, and then to implement your own version of the system as you make a second pass over the material in each chapter.

---

[1] For example, if changes are made to a definition ('.h') module, all implementation files that #include that file need to be compiled again.

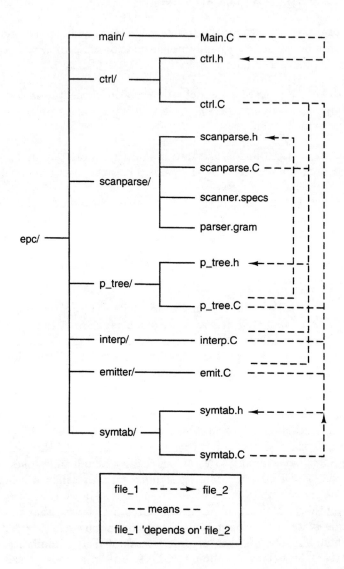

Figure 3.2. Directory Structure

Execution Milestone	File and specific contents.
1.	ctrl.h ctrl.C (simple constructor)
2.	main.C ctrl.C (extented ctr, file capability, create scanner obj) scanparse.C (simple def and impl of scanparse class)
3.	parser.gram (the tokens and single production) scanner.specs parser.gram (complete grammar) ctrl.C (add call to parser)
4.	ptree.h ptree.C parser.gram (to create the tree) ctrl.C (to reference the parse tree)
5.	symtab.h symtab.C ptree.C (tree nodes which reference symtab)
6.	interp.C emit.C ctrl.C (send messages to interpret or emit)

Figure 3.3. Scheduling the System's Development

3.2.3 Makefiles

Keeping track of the various file dependencies and corresponding executed commands is at best an unpleasant task on a project the size of the elementary compiler and an impossibility on a medium size project such as the complete Pascal compiler. Fortunately almost all operating systems have a utility such as *make*, that enables a programmer to maintain up-to-date versions of the various modules and to invoke automatically the correct executable commands needed to (re)create any of the modules that may need updating. For purposes of illustration, this text uses the specific syntax for the UNIX *make* utility.

Make determines file dependency by constructing a dependency tree based upon a specification file, called *Makefile*. Any file that depends on another file that has a later access time will automatically be selected for a re*make*. There are three kinds of items in a Makefile: macros, dependencies, and commands. Macros are just abbreviations for strings to be used throughout the Makefile. Macros often

```
┌─────────────────────────────────────────────────────────────────────┐
│  ┌──────────┐                                                         │
│  │ Makefile │                                                         │
│  └──────────┘                                                         │
│    1    # Makefile for Example Pascal Compiler                        │
│    2                                                                   │
│    3    SUBDIR  =   main ctrl scanparse p_tree interp emitter symtab  │
│    4                                                                   │
│    5    DOTOHS  =   ctrl/ctrl.o scanparse/scanparse.o p_tree/p_tree.o\ │
│    6                interp/interp.o emitter/emit.o symtab/symtab.o main/Main.o│
│    7                                                                   │
│    8    PROGRAM:                                                       │
│    9            for i in ${SUBDIR}; do \                               │
│   10                    (echo $$i;cd $$i; make;); \                    │
│   11            done                                                   │
│   12            CC -o epc $(DOTOHS)                                    │
│   13                                                                   │
│   14    clean:                                                         │
│   15            for i in ${SUBDIR}; do \                               │
│   16                    (echo $$i;cd $$i; make clean;); \              │
│   17            done                                                   │
│   18            rm -f *.o tmp* a.out epc                               │
│   19    print:                                                         │
│   20            /usr/5bin/pr -n Main.C Makefile > Example_comp.lst     │
│   21            a2ps Example_comp.lst | lpr -Pmlw                      │
│   22            rm -f *.lst                                            │
│   23            for i in ${SUBDIR}; do \                               │
│   24                    (echo $$i;cd $$i; make print;); \              │
│   25            done                                                   │
│   26                                                                   │
│   27    count:                                                         │
│   28            for i in ${SUBDIR}; do \                               │
│   29                    (echo $$i;cd $$i; make count;); \              │
│   30            done                                                   │
└─────────────────────────────────────────────────────────────────────┘
```

take the form

$$FILECOLLECTION = file1 \; file2 \; file3$$

so that a long string of file names can be easily referenced later in the *make* specification file. Dependencies are specified by a line of the form

$$file1: \quad file2 \; file3 \; file4$$

indicating that file1 depends on file2, file3 and file4. Commands that are to be taken to make the various modules are placed immediately after a dependency line. They often look like

$$Command < switches > file1 \ldots filen$$

where the command is a system call to either a compiler or a linker.

Make is an extremely flexible utility. Each programmer usually develops a particular *make* style, much like each programmer develops a unique style using a particular editor. One approach, often used at the early stages of a project is hierarchical: Put a high-level *Makefile* in the outer directory (Figure 3.2), that calls individual *makefiles* in the various subdirectories. As subdirectories come and go, the wear and tear on the programmer seems to be less this way.

A *makefile* for the outer *epc* directory is on page 22. As noted earlier, the line numbers have been included only for reference and are not part of the actual file. Remember, that this is a later version of the file. Initial versions might contain references only to the main module or the controller. The *makefile* contains two macros. Line 3 defines a macro SUBDIR consisting of the subdirectories used in the embryo project; the macro in Line 5 just lists all the ".o" files, which are linked to create the executable.

The loop structure simply goes into each of the subdirectories and executes the corresponding makefile for each module. The specific module makefiles are listed at the end of each of the corresponding chapters of this workbook.

Line 12 contains the command to link all the object files. The −o option directs the compiler to rename the executable file *a.out* to *epc*.

Lines 14 and 19 contain little tricks used by some programmers. The command *make clean* will cause *make* to perform the *make clean* command in each of the subdirectories, allowing a fresh start or the simulation of building the system from scratch. *Make print* is an example of the type of commands used to make listings of programs. The UNIX utility *pr* formats the listings. The ASCII-to-postscript utility *a2ps* may not be universally available; the printer *mlw* is just a local printer; yours will undoubtedly be called something else.

3.3 Summary

In this chapter we have described the following items.

- A short list of the specific behaviors of the compiler. You will probably want to modify the list given to include an additional Pascal statement, or to allow for modes of interaction more appropriate to your own computing platform.

- An object-oriented software development strategy.

- An initial design effort at specifying the various modules.

- A list of the directories for the example compiler.

- The use of *make* to help manage the development of the system. In particular, we have discussed the contents of a makefile and the use of make for a system that involves subdirectories.

3.4 Suggested Activities

1. It may be helpful to explore the capabilities of an existing compiler before you begin the analysis and design of your own system. This question is designed to raise a number of issues for your consideration.

   Locate an existing compiler and corresponding documentation on your system.

   (a) Most compilers have an option displaying the highest level compilation commands used during a normal session. On many compilers this is a - *dryrun* switch. Using this feature, make a list of the sequence of activities normally performed by your compiler.

   (b) Is your compiler a multipass compiler? If so, what tasks are performed on each pass? It may be possible to watch this by putting a compiling job in the back ground and then running a system-watch program. If so, approximately how much time does each pass take?

   (c) Does your compiler have an optimizer? Write a simple program that is fairly compute-bound, e.g., nested iterations executing a selection statement. Compare the performance of regularly compiled code with that which as been optimized.

   (d) Scan the list of compiler options and make a list of those you would like to include in your compiler. In particular, what kind of print options are important?

   (e) Place an intentional error in a source program.
   - How are lexical errors reported?
   - How are syntax errors indicated?

   (f) Is there an interpreter available? How is it used? Compare time performance of interpreted programs with compiled programs.

   (g) A pretty printer reformats the source program, based upon the syntax of the source program and subject to various style options. Pretty printers can be implemented as a part of the compiler system or as a separate program.
      i. Pretty print a number of language constructs: iteration statements, control statements, subprogram declarations, etc.
      ii. What formatting options are available?

   (h) What kind of debugging aids does your compiler provide?
      i. What options are possible for range checking of array indices?
      ii. Use the system debugger to trace a simple program.
      iii. A profiler counts the number of times that certain subprograms or structures are executed. Profile a simple program containing multiple calls to a particular subprogram.

2. Prepare a simple analysis document for your own compiler:

   (a) Write a description of the system you would like to build. Include possible extensions to the description in this chapter. Adding a looping statement or an additional data type is an excellent project.

   (b) Make a list of important objects and classes for your compiler.

   (c) Specify the format for input to your compiler. Do the same for compiler output.

3. Design and build a directory structure suitable for your own version of the compiler. You may want to do this incrementally, adding subdirectories only as needed.

4. Construct a makefile for the outer level directory that calls corresponding makefiles for each of the subdirectories. A sample subdirectory makefile is listed below.

```
┌─────────────────────────────────────────────────┐
│ │Minimal subdirectory makefile│                   │
│                                                   │
│ PROGRAM:                                          │
│            pwd                                    │
│            ls -l                                  │
└─────────────────────────────────────────────────┘
```

It contains no macros, no dependencies, and only requests that the commands be executed that print the working (sub)directory and output a detailed (long) listing of the included files.

Chapter 4

Main()

4.1 C++ Main Function

A system implemented in C++ must contain a driver function *main()* (Stroustrup [12, page 81]) to which program control is transferred immediately after normal system initialization is completed. A C++ listing of *Main.C* for the example compiler is given below.

```
(Main.C)

 1 /*
 2  *      Main.C  -- For Example Compiler
 3  */
 4
 5 #include <iostream.h>
 6
 7 #include "../ctrl/ctrl.h"
 8
 9 main(int argc, char** argv) {
10     //cout << " Example Pascal compiler" << endl;
11
12     PControllerCls ctl = new ControllerCls(argc,argv);
13 }
```

4.2 C++ Concepts

There are a number of elementary ideas about C++[1] that can be noted from *Main.C*.

Comments. Any characters between /* and */ are ignored by the C++ compiler. Any characters occurring on a line after the symbol // are also considered comments. Over the years we have adopted a convention of placing an output statement

---

[1] Trying to describe C++ is like shooting at a moving target. The language, though essentially quite stable, still is undergoing an evolution. The descriptions of C++ capabilities and limitations found in this text and in *Object-Oriented Compiler Construction* are based on AT&T's version 2.0, which is widely used and well documented (e.g., Lippman [8]).

in each function that may be turned off by a comment. In a number of C++ systems, the standard debuggers are unable to accurately trace back to the original source file. Having some method of identifying the underlying class of a given object is important, especially when dealing with many objects from various subclasses. If your C++ compiling system supports a solid dynamic debugger, then you certainly would not need such identifying statements.

Preprocessor directives. Any line beginning with a # is actually a compiler directive. Directives are processed prior to the actual compilation process. The program that usually handles these directives is called a **preprocessor**. The line

$$\#include \; < iostream.h >$$

directs the preprocessor to include the definitions of classes in the standard header file *iostream.h*, a file usually found in a commonly accessed directory and supporting normal input and output.

Since the task of *main()* is to construct a controller object, the only local module imported is *ctrl.h*, located in the *ctrl subdirectory* and explained in more detail in Section 5.1.

Output and input. In most modern programming languages the mechanisms for performing input or output are not a part of the actual language definition. Instead, the details are often implemented as a library that is made available for use by #includeing the definitions and linking the implementations. The library for C++ is called *iostream*. This library is divided into two levels. The low level is a collection of classes that are responsible for putting or getting characters. The upper level contains (among others) two classes *istream* and *ostream*, that are responsible for formatting the input and output. There are four streams that are predefined and available to the user. The three most important ones are described below.

cout Output directed from the user's terminal is usually called **standard output**. *Cout* is an instance of the ostream class. Information is moved from a program to the standard output device by means of the **insertion** operator <<, as illustrated in the line

```
cout << "Example Pascal compiler" ;
```

Endl is called a **manipulator** because its use causes a particular action to be performed on the ostream. In this case a newline is inserted into the ostream and the stream buffer is flushed of its contents.

cin Input directed to the user's terminal is usually called **standard input**. Information is moved from the standard input device to the user program by using the predefined istream object *cin* and the **extraction** operator >>, as shown in the following example.

```
cin >> x;
```

It turns out that this object is not as useful in compiler writing, since most input is done through the scanner and most generated scanners use input *functions* that are defined in the C library *stdio*. We discuss this at more length in Chapter 5

cerr This third predefined ostream is used to alert the user to some exceptional condition in the program during execution. Information is also placed in this stream by the insertion operator.

Command line arguments. Users can initially communicate with most programs by setting options or specifying a file name after invoking the program. This *command line* communication often takes the following form.

$$epc - l \ prog.p$$

In a UNIX environment these extra pieces of information are made available to the function *main()* through the two arguments *argc* and *argv*, what are indicated on Line 9 of the *Main.C* listing. The first argument indicates the number of command line strings available for access by *main()*; the second is a pointer to a string[2] containing the actual commands. These two arguments are then passed to the constructor for the ControllerCls object which then modifies the behavior of the compiler, based upon the contents of the arguments.

Pointers. The first few lines from *ctrl.h* (Chapter 5)

```
typedef ControllerCls *PControllerCls;
class ControllerCls {
```

indicate that *PControllerCls* is just another name for *ControllerCls**, a *pointer* to a *ControllerCls*. In *Main.C*, the expression

$$PControllerCls \ ctl = new \ ControllerCls(argc, argv);$$

is therefore defining *ctl* to be a pointer whose value is the address of a *ControllerCls* object that has been constructed by the C++ *new* operator.

4.3   Makefile

Since the only `include` in *main.C* is for the controller, *Main.o* depends on the controller's *.h* and the implementation source *Main.C*. The *-g* option allows the use of a debugging program on many systems.

---

[2]Note that C++ is just like C in its use of the * operator for type declaration: A variable of type *char** is either a pointer to a char (possibly, even a contiguous string of chars) or perhaps a pointer to the first entry of an array of char. Clearly, *char * ** could be a number of somewhat equivalent types. In the case of command line arguments, *argv* is a pointer to an array of strings.

```
(main/Makefile)

 1 # Makefile for Main module
 2
 3 PROGRAM:           Main.o
 4
 5 Main.o:            ../ctrl/ctrl.h Main.C
 6                    CC -c -g Main.C
 7
 8 clean:
 9                    rm -f *.o tmp* a.out epc
10
11 print:
12                    /usr/5bin/pr -n Main.C Makefile > Example_comp.lst
13                    a2ps Example_comp.lst | lpr -Pmlw
14                    rm -f *.lst
15 count:
16                    wc *.C Makefile
```

4.4 Summary

We have introduced the following ideas in this chapter.

- C++ format for *main()*. Also included is a description of C++ facilities for passing command level arguments to the program via the variables *argc* and *argv*.

- Sample makefile for *main()*.

4.5 Suggested Activities

1. Implement your own version of *main()*. If you have not yet worked on the *ctrl* module, comment out any reference to *ControllerCls*.

2. If your operating system supports command line communication,

   (a) Experiment with the program *main()* from Activity 1 by:
       - Adding instructions to *main()* that will print out the values of *argc*, **argv* and ***argv*.
       - Executing main with no extra command line arguments. Note the value of *argc* and *argv*. Then repeat with first one and then several arguments.

   (b) Write a C++ program that prints out the sum of any string of integers input through the command line.

Chapter 5

System Control

5.1 Controller Module

Traditional procedurally oriented programming methods often manage the timing of crucial events in a very natural and almost effortless way. Since the focus is on algorithms and their relation to various (sub)procedures, the sequence of events often follows automatically from the implementation of those algorithms.

Object-oriented design and programming methods focus primarily on the *specification* of subsystems or classes. Timing of events often requires special analysis and design and special control objects to coordinate the sequencing of events, particularly the creating of important objects.

The module described in this section consists of two files *ctrl.h* and *ctrl.C*, illustrated in Figure 5.1, that contain the definition and implementation of classes controlling the behavior of the Pascal compiler. The class definition file contains specifications for two classes which are concerned with system management.

- **OptionCls**.

  OptionCls manages compiler option information selected by the user. It contains data members for storing the selected options and a member function which allow other compiler components access to the option information.

- **ControllerCls**.

  ControllerCls creates the various compiler objects and coordinates their behaviors. Actually, it is the *constructor* of the class that performs the various controller functions.

5.1.1 Header

Our standard practice in this text is to first list the various class dependencies or `#includes`. This allows us to discuss the definition and implementation of each of the various classes. Next, the appropriate class definition will be printed from the *.h* file. Finally, the corresponding class implementation is listed from the *.C* file. Indicated line numbers should serve to orient the location of the code in the various files. If not, the listings in Appendix A will provide the necessary context.

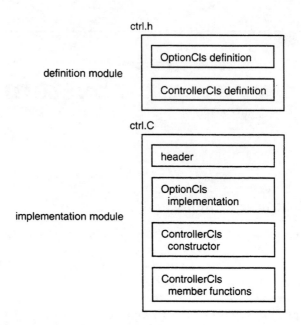

Figure 5.1. Structure of *ctrl* Module

The following listing contains C++ header code for *ctrl.C*.

```
Header Section(ctrl.C)

 1 /* header */
 2 /*
 3 *        ctrl.C  ControllerCls  Implementation Module
 4 */
 5
 6 #include <iostream.h>
 7 #include <stdio.h>
 8 #include <string.h>
 9
10 #include "../scanparse/scanparse.h"
11 #include "../p_tree/p_tree.h"
12 #include "../symtab/symtab.h"
13
14 #include "ctrl.h"
```

Stdio.h and *string.h* (lines 7 and 8) contain functions used in Section 5.1.3, below. Since the controller must have access to the other major parts of the compiler, the controller must **include** the definitions of the various classes found in the modules for the scanner/parser, the parse tree and the symbol table (lines 10–12).

5.1.2   OptionCls

OptionCls stores and provides information on the user selected options.

```
OptionCls Definition(ctrl.h)

 5 typedef class OptionCls *POptionCls;
 6 class OptionCls {
 7    public:
 8          static int option_info();
 9          friend class ControllerCls;
10    private:
11          OptionCls();        //Called only by ControllerCls
12          static int    list;
13          static int    emit;
14 };
```

The general features of a class definition are clearly seen in this code. Essentially a class definition is just a specification of various kinds of members. Some members are functions; some members are data or class attributes. Lines 10–13 of the definition of *OptionCls* specify that the class constructor *OptionCls()* and the two option attributes *list* and *emit* are hidden from all client objects, except a *friend* class like *ControllerCls*.

Line 8 uses *static* to describe a special kind of function, that is associated with the *class* rather than particular objects of that class. Any other object is thus able to determine which options have been set by requesting information by using a command like [*OptionCls* :: *option_info*(); rather than the more customary *opt* → *option_info*(); that requires that an instance *opt* of class *OptionCls* be created first.

```
OptionCls Implementation (ctrl.C)

20 OptionCls :: OptionCls() {
21      //cout << "OptionCls() " << endl;
22      list = 0;
23      emit = 0;
24 }
25
26 int OptionCls :: option_info() {
27      return (list | emit);
28 }
```

These implementation details contain very few new C++ ideas. The *OptionCls* constructor initializes the attributes *list* and *emit*. The function *option_info()* returns the (integer value of the) bitwise OR of the option attributes. Line 21 is just another example of an output statement that can be used to test order of execution if necessary.

5.1.3   ControllerCls

ControllerCls is responsible for coordinating the timing of the events in the compiler.

```
ControllerCls Definition(ctrl.h)

17 class SymtabCls;  // 'forward'
18 class PTreeCls;   //       references
19
20 typedef class ControllerCls *PControllerCls;
21 class ControllerCls {
22    public:
23         ControllerCls(int argc, char** argv);
24         void            print();
25    private:
26         SymtabCls       *std_table;
27         PTreeCls        *parse_tree;
28         int             open_file(char*);
29 };
```

The code listed above contains the definition of *ControllerCls*. There are two C++ ideas worth noting in this code.

- The first two statements in the definition of *ControllerCls* are just forward references to classes that are associated with *ControllerCls*. These statements tell the C++ compiler CC not to get too concerned with references to *SymtabCls* and *PTreeCls*, since these classes will be defined and implemented in another module.

- The (non*friendl*y) function *main()* in *Main.C* creates the *ControllerCls* object for the compiler. The *ControllerCls* constructor has therefore been made **publ**ically accessible.

- Conventional wisdom in the world of C is that extensive use of pointers is a sign of efficient programming. Certainly it is much faster to send an address into a function than a complex data structure. But there is an even more significant object-oriented reason for pointer use: The indication of class relationships. Clearly, objects within a system are useful primarily if they interact with other objects in ways prescribed by the designer. Object interaction is most often prescribed at design time in terms of **relationships** between the corresponding classes. Of the many kinds of class relationships, only two are extensively used in the example compiler.

    - The **subclass** relationship.

      This relationship is often called **inheritance**, since the subclass inherits the attributes of the main class. We describe this relationship in Chapter 8, page 81.

– The **uses** relationship.

This second important class relationship specifies that a class instance "uses" or sends a messages to another object. Such relationships are often specified as pointers in the data member section of a class definition. The class definition above is therefore specifying that a *ControllerCls* object needs to communicate with a *SymtabCls* and a *PTreeCls* object.

The *ControllerCls* object is responsible for monitoring the compiler's options and for keeping track of the default symbol table and the root of the parse tree. As noted earlier, these links between objects are implemented by storing pointers to those objects.

The following implementation code for *ControllerCls* in *ctrl.C* does contain ideas of note. The compiler's symbol table and rudimentary *ScopeCls* (Chapter 7) object (for keeping track of the scope of variables) are created. *Argc* in Line 64 gives information about the number of command line arguments passed to the compiler. As long as there are options and a source file name specified, the *for*(...){... } loop processes the information.

Line 90 calls the *ControllerCls* member function *open_file()*; if it returns true, then the following items occur.

- In Line 91 the normal C input/output package *stdio* used by the scanner is synchronized with the C++ *stream* objects *cin* and *cout*.

- Line 92 creates a ScanParseCls object **sp*. The *ScanParseCls* constructor (see Chapter 6) actually performs the entire parsing process.

- The *parse_tree* link to the tree generated by the parser in Line 92 is placed in the appropriate attribute in Line 93. The use of the C++ keyword *this* in this context is primarily an aid to programmer understanding. *This* is a pointer to the controller object. We use it in our programming primarily to remind the programmer that *parse_tree* is a data member of *ControllerCls*.

- Lines 95–99 give commands to emit code or interpret the program. In a more mature compiler, these lines would be executed only if no syntax or semantic errors had been detected at Line 92. Since this compiler requires a correct 'Pascal' source program, either *emit()* or *execute()* will always be performed.

ControllerCls Implementation (ctrl.C)

```
 54 ControllerCls :: ControllerCls(int argc, char** argv) {
 55     //cout << "ControllerCls() " << endl;
 56
 57
 58     this -> std_table = new SymtabCls;
 59     PScopeCls scp = new ScopeCls;
 60     scp -> vista = this -> std_table;
 61
 62     char *source_file = new char[80];
 63     this -> parse_tree = 0;
 64     if (argc <= 1) {
 65         cout << "        Usage:  epc [-el] <filename>.p" << endl;
 66         return;
 67     } else {
 68         for (int i = 1; i < argc; i++) {
 69             if (*argv[i] == '-') {
 70                 while (*++argv[i]) {
 71                     switch(*argv[i]) {
 72                     case 'l':
 73                         OptionCls :: list = 1;
 74                         continue;
 75
 76                     case 'e':
 77                         OptionCls :: emit = 2;
 78                         continue;
 79
 80                     default:
 81                         cerr << "Unknown option " <<
 82                                         *argv[i] << endl;
 83                     }
 84                 }
 85             } else {
 86                 source_file = argv[i];
 87             }
 88         }
 89     }
 90     if (open_file(source_file)) {
 91         ios::sync_with_stdio();
 92         PScanParseCls sp = new ScanParseCls;
 93         this -> parse_tree = sp -> parse_tree;
 94
 95         if (OptionCls::emit) {
 96             parse_tree -> emit();
 97         } else {
 98             parse_tree -> execute();
 99         }
100     }
101 }
```

ControllerCls member function.   The implementation code for the *ControllerCls* member function *open_file()* is listed below.

```
(ctrl.C)

30 int  ControllerCls :: open_file(char* source_file) {
31     //cout << "ControllerCls::open_file()" << source_file << endl;
32     int length = strlen(source_file);
33     //Check for  .p  extension
34     if ((length > 1) && ((source_file[length -2] == '.') &&
35                          (source_file[length -1] == 'p')  )) {
36         if (!freopen(source_file, "r", stdin)) {
37             cout << "   Cannot open file -- Sorry " << endl;
38             //should be done by an ErrorCls object
39             return 0;
40         } else {
41             return 1;
42         }
43     } else if (length == 0) {
44         cout << "       No file specified" << endl;
45         return 0;
46     } else {
47         cout << "        File must have a  .p  extension" << endl;
48         //should be done by an ErrorCls object
49         return 0;
50     }
51 }
```

This function accepts a string *source_file* as its argument and returns an *int* value of 1 (or 0) indicating the success or failure of opening the source file in preparation for scanning. Several lines contain noteworthy items.

- Line 32: The function *strlen()* comes from the system string library, *string.h*, and returns the length of a null-terminated string.

- Line 36: The normal input channel used by the scanner is switched from *stdin* (the keyboard) to the indicated source file. *Freopen* opens a file using an existing file variable. The rationale behind *freopen* is that a new file can be associated with a stream without informing all those having copies of the stream value. This provides a nice way to disassociate either *stdin* or *stdout* from the console and associate it with a chosen file.

- Lines 43–50: Pascal source files should have the usual *.p* extension, even for the example compiler.

5.2   Module Makefile

```
ctrl/Makefile

   1 PROGRAM:          ctrl.h ctrl.o
   2
   3 ctrl.o: ../scanparse/scanparse.h ../p_tree/p_tree.h \
   4         ../symtab/symtab.h ctrl.h ctrl.C
   5         CC -c -g ctrl.C
   6
   7 clean:
   8         rm -f  *.o a.out
   9
  10 print:
  11         /usr/5bin/pr -n ctrl.h ctrl.C Makefile > Ctrl.lst
  12         a2ps Ctrl.lst | lpr -Pmlw
  13         rm -f Ctrl.lst
  14
  15 count:
  16         wc *.h *.C Makefile
```

5.3   Summary

This chapter has presented information about the following items.

- Discussion of initial design decisions for controller module.

- Definition and Implementation details for *OptionCls*.

- Definition and implementation details of *ControllerCls*.

5.4   Suggested Activities

1. Implement your own versions of *ctrl.h* and *ctrl.C*. Again, you will want to comment out any references to classes that have not yet been defined or implemented. You will have arrived at the first execution milestone when you complete the coding and testing of the various classes in this module.

2. The content of a *.h* (include) file is always a matter requiring some discussion or even debate. Question: Why not put all the messy header information contained in the *ctrl.C* header section into the *ctrl.h* and then import it into *ctrl.C* with the single line *#include"ctrl.h"*?

3. (Possible Extension)

   (a) Modify the definition of *OptionCls* to include a run-time semantic check option -*C*. This option might check that integer values never exceeded some very modest MAXINT value. Normally, such an option would also check that array indices remain within defined index limits, and that variables declared as a subrange type remain within the subrange boundaries. Since the compiler has only the single type *integer* and this is automatically declared, it really is not possible to impose these more nontrivial semantic restrictions.

(b) Make the corresponding modifications to the *OptionCls* implementation code to provide for the new option.

(c) Make modifications to the *ControllerCls* constructor so that the option is detected and the corresponding option value is set.

(d) Test that the *-C* option is actually detected by *ControllerCls*.

Chapter 6

The Scanner/Parser Module

Before we begin to look at code, let's list a number of important scanner/parser facts.

- Lexemes are "chunks" of Pascal source code.

- Tokens are integers that represent categories of various lexemes.

- The scanner does the following things.

  - Breaks the source file into lexemes.
  - Determines the corresponding token and returns it to the parser.
  - Places line number information into a LexTokCls object.

- The parser does the following things.

  - Invokes the scanner.
  - Checks source code syntax using tokens from scanner.
  - Creates a parse tree representing the source program.

- The parse tree does the following things (among others).

  - Stores relevant lexeme and line number information from LexTokCls objects.
  - Checks the few Pascal semantic requirements that the example compiler must enforce.

6.1 The Encapsulator: ScanparseCls

The *scanparse* module provides the compiler's scanning and parsing services as well as facilities for inter- and intramodule object communication. This module is in the usual two pieces, *scanparse.h* and *scanparse.C*, as illustrated in Figure 6.1, although additional files such as *scanner.specs* (for the scanner function *yylex()*, Section 6.2) and *parser.gram* (for the parser function *yyparse()*, Section 6.3), are also used in the construction of *scanparse.C*.

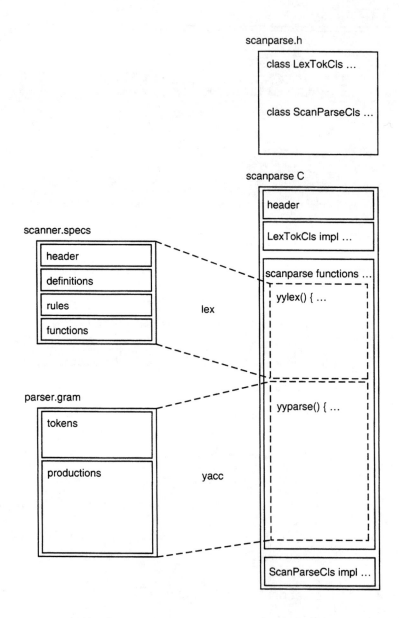

Figure 6.1. Layout of ScanParseCls Module

6.1.1 Scanparse Header

```
ScanParseCls Header (scanparse.C)

6 //      header
7 #include <stream.h>
8 #include "../p_tree/p_tree.h"
9 #include "scanparse.h"
```

This is the header for the implementation file of the scanparse module. Since the parser actually constructs the parse tree during the parsing phase, the definitions of the classes for the parse tree nodes must be #included as in line 8.[1] These definitions are described in Chapter 8. The definitions of the various scanner/parser classes are #included in line 9 so that their implementations can be coded.

6.1.2 LexTokCls

LexTokCls provides convenient communication between the scanner and error reporting objects used in later stages of compiler development. The parse tree often needs explicit lexeme information when checking semantics; *LexTokCls* objects are the medium of exchange for that information.

Definition. The following class definition contains three rather obvious private members and two public member functions, including a constructor.

```
LexTokCls Definition (scanparse.h)

 5 typedef class LexTokCls *PLexTokCls;
 6 class LexTokCls {
 7   public:
 8        LexTokCls(int LineNo, int Token, char *Lexeme);
 9        char*  get_lexeme() {return lexeme;}
10   private:
11        int    line_no;
12        char   *lexeme;
13        int    token;
14 };
15
```

Implementation. The following listing contains the class implementation details for *LexTokCls*.

---

[1]If you are using *yacc* (Section 6.3), rather than *byacc*, you may also need to #include the definitions in the file *malloc.h*.

```
(LexTokCls Implementation (scanparse.C))

12 #include <string.h>
13 LexTokCls :: LexTokCls(int LineNo, int Token, char *Lexeme) {
14     //cout << "LexTokCls(LineNo, Token, Lexeme)" << endl;
15     line_no = LineNo;
16     token   = Token;
17     lexeme = new char[80];
18     if (Lexeme) {
19         strcpy(lexeme,Lexeme);
20     }
21 }
```

The library function *strcpy()* is defined in the system library *string.h*; it is used
in line 19 to avoid aliasing of strings. Aliasing is a situation where one single copy
of the actual string data is being referenced by many variables. *Strcpy* actually
makes a separate copy of the incoming lexeme value so that distinct *LexTokCls*
objects have their own lexeme space.

6.1.3   Scanparse Functions

The following listing #includes the major portion of the scanner/parser module.

```
Functions Included (scanparse.C)

24 PPTreeNodeCls prgm_node; //Global!
25         //Set by top of tree, ProgramCls.
26 #include "scanparse.fct"
```

Scanparse.fct is the fairly large file, illustrated in Figure 6.1, consisting of C code
for the scanner and the parser. The details of the construction of this file are found
in Sections 6.2 and 6.3, below.

6.1.4   ScanParseCls

Definition.   The definition in the following code contains very few new C++ ideas.

```
ScanParseCls Definition (scanparse.h)

17 class PTreeCls;
18
19 typedef class ScanParseCls *PScanParseCls;
20 class ScanParseCls {
21   public:
22         ScanParseCls();
23         void        print();
24         friend class ControllerCls;
25   private:
26         PTreeCls    *parse_tree;
27 };
```

The public member function *print*() is really an antibugging device. During compilation, it is useful to have the various structures print themselves. Also notice the existence of a class association; the link between the *ScanParseCls* object and the corresponding *PTreeCls* object is implemented by use of the pointer *parse_tree*.

Implementation.   There is one noteworthy point in the following constructor.

```
ScanParseCls Implementation (scanparse.C)

28 ScanParseCls :: ScanParseCls() {
29     //cout << "ScanParseCls()" << endl;
30     yyparse();
31     parse_tree = new PTreeCls(prgm_node);
32 }
```

The *ScanParseCls* constructor actually begins the parsing process by calling the parsing function *yyparse*() in line 30. As soon as all parsing action is complete, the parse tree root, that is stored in the global *prgm_node* (see code in Section 6.1.3), is then attached to the *parse_tree* member of *ScanParseCls*.

6.2   The Scanner: yylex()

6.2.1   Tokens

The scanner and parser need to cooperate on a number of fronts, one of which is the list of tokens. Two separate lists of token definitions are clearly not satisfactory. *Lex* and *yacc* handle this problem by allowing a specification of the token names in the parser declaration *parser.gram*, which is then converted (Figure 6.2) into a token declaration file *y.tab.h* available for #includeing into the scanner. So if we place the following set of tokens in *parser.gram*,

```
List of tokens (parser.gram)

10 %token PROGRAMTK
11 %token BEGINTK
12 %token ENDTK
13 %token SCTK
14 %token ASGTK
15 %token DOTTK
16 %token IDENTIFIERTK
17 %token NUMLITERALTK
18 %token WRITETK
19 %token LPARENTK
20 %token RPARENTK
```

the *yacc -d* command illustrated in Figure 6.2 will convert them into the following token definitions.

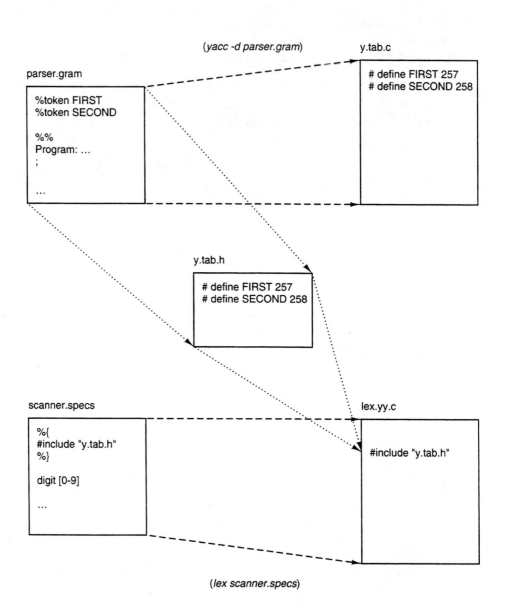

Figure 6.2. Producing and Using Tokens

```
Token Definitions (y.tab.h)

 1 #define PROGRAMTK 257
 2 #define BEGINTK 258
 3 #define ENDTK 259
 4 #define SCTK 260
 5 #define ASGTK 261
 6 #define DOTTK 262
 7 #define IDENTIFIERTK 263
 8 #define NUMLITERALTK 264
 9 #define WRITETK 265
10 #define LPARENTK 266
11 #define RPARENTK 267
```

This information can then be #included into any file needing token information.

6.2.2 Scanner Specification File

As illustrated in Figure 6.1 the UNIX utility *lex* produces a scanner from the information found in a scanner specification file. This file consists of a header, a set of lexeme definitions, a set of scanning rules, and a collection of user-supplied functions.

Header section
Lexeme regular expressions
%%
Scanner rules
%%
User-defined supporting functions

Header.   The header for the scanner specification file is listed below.

```
(scanner.specs)

 1 %{
 2 /*
 3 *        scanner.specs
 4 */
 5
 6 #include "y.tab.h"
 7
 8 #include "../ctrl/ctrl.h"
 9 PLexTokCls lex_tok;
10
11 %}
```

Note that the file of tokens *y.tab.h* is #included. The *ControllerCls* definition module *ctrl.h* is also imported to allow access to the definition of *OptionCls*. line 9 is a (module-wide) global pointing to the *LextokCls* object corresponding to the lexeme currently being recognized by the scanner.

Lexeme definitions. Lexemes that the scanner recognizes are specified using a very natural kind of symbolism called **regular expressions**. A valid Pascal digit could be represented by

$$\{0, 1, 2, 3, 4, 5, 6, 7, 8, 9\}$$

but the extended regular expression notation

$$[0 - 9]$$

used in the following specification

```
Scanner Regular Expressions (scanner.specs)

13 digit            [0-9]
14 digits           {digit}+
15 letter           [A-Za-z]
16 letter_or_digit  ({letter}|{digit})
17 ident            {letter}{letter_or_digit}*
18 whitespace       [ \t]
19 cr               [\n]
20 other
```

is certainly much easier to write and to read. Similar comments apply to the definition of *letter* as

$$[A - Za - z]$$

where the juxtaposition of the two ranges $A - Z$ and $a - z$ indicates an *or* operation.

The + in line 14 indicates a repetition of one or more of the preceding items; in this case *digits* is therefore defined as one or more digits. The * in line 17 denotes a repetition of zero or more of the preceding items. A valid Pascal *identifier* (or even a reserved word) is therefore specified to be a letter followed by zero or more *letter_or_digits*.

Scanner rules. This section of the scanner specification file indicates the *actions* that the scanner should perform when it recognizes a lexeme matching one of the definitions above.

```
┌─────────────────────────────┐
│ Scanner Rules (scanner.specs) │
└─────────────────────────────┘
   24 {whitespace}    {ckout();}
   25
   26 {cr}            {ckout();}
   27
   28
   29 ";"             {ckout();
   30                  lex_tok = new LexTokCls(yylineno, SCTK, 0);
   31                  return SCTK;}
   32
   33 "("             {ckout();
   34                  lex_tok = new LexTokCls(yylineno, LPARENTK, 0);
   35                  return LPARENTK;}
   36
   37 ")"             {ckout();
   38                  lex_tok = new LexTokCls(yylineno, RPARENTK, 0);
   39                  return RPARENTK;}
   40
   41 ":="            {ckout();
   42                  lex_tok = new LexTokCls(yylineno, ASGTK, 0);
   43                  return ASGTK;}
   44
   45 "."             {ckout();
   46                  lex_tok = new LexTokCls(yylineno, DOTTK, 0);
   47                  return DOTTK;}
   48
   49 {digits}    {ckout();
   50              lex_tok = new LexTokCls(yylineno, NUMLITERALTK, yytext);
   51              return NUMLITERALTK;}
   52
   53 {ident}     {ckout();
   54              int actual_tk = ck_reserved_wd();
   55              lex_tok = new LexTokCls(yylineno, actual_tk, yytext);
   56              return actual_tk;}
   57
   58 {other}     {ckout();
   59              return yytext[0];}
```

The above rules specify that the following scanning actions be taken when the indicated category of lexeme is recognized.

- White spaces and carriage returns are ignored, except in the event that a user requests a source listing. The actual code of the function *ckout()*, responsible for producing the listing of the Pascal source file, is listed below.

- Special one-character lexemes are recognized and their tokens returned to the parser. The zero argument is passed to the *LexTokCls* constructor, since the ASCII character value can always be deduced from the token value.

- The character string lexeme values for numeric literals is available (line 50) in the global *yytext*.

- Identifiers *and* reserved words are recognized by the same rule. This strange arrangement is actually a clever way of improving the performance and reducing the size of the scanner suggested by Schreiner and Friedman [10]. Rather than making a separate rule for each Pascal reserved word, all potential reserved words are first recognized as *identifiers* and then sent to an efficient reserved-word checker *ck_reserved_wd()* (line 54), that passes back the appropriate token value.

- Anything not specified by the scanner rules will be recognized as *other* and sent as such to the parser, which is responsible for sending appropriate error messages in more mature versions of the compiler.

User-supplied functions. As a scanner is built, specialized behavior is often necessary when a particular lexeme is recognized. The most famous of these functions occurs in scanning languages allowing nesting of comments,where it is necessary to read the input stream character by character until the outermost comment terminator is encountered. This last section of the scanner specification file allows a convenient location for the declaration of such functions.

In our little compiler, we really only need two such function.

- *ckout()*

- *ck_reserved_wd()*

The next listing is the C++ code for the function *ckout()*, which produces listings during the compilation of source programs.

```
Scanner Does Listing (scanner.specs)

63 #include <string.h>
64 char *textline = new char[257];
65
66 void ckout() {
67     textline = strcat(textline,yytext);
68     if (yytext[0] == '\n') {
69         if (OptionCls::option_info() % 2) {  //List option is a 1
70             cout << "[";
71             cout.width(5);
72             cout <<  yylineno -1 << "]      " << textline ;
73         }
74         textline[0] = '\0';
75     }
76 }
```

The present version of *ckout()*, which accumulates the reserved lexemes, uses the concatenation operator *strcat()* from the string library *string.h* to collect the lexemes until a newline character is encountered. *Ckout()* then outputs the reconstructed source line.

Yytext and *yylineno* are scanner globals, encapsulated in the *scanparse* module. Also, the instruction **cout.width(5)** is just C++ code for formatting the width of integer valued output produced by the *cout* instruction immediately following.

The ideas for the next two pieces of code have been gleaned from Schreiner and Friedman [10].

```
  Reserved Words (scanner.specs)

  78 struct rwtable_str {
  79     char *rw_name;       /* lexeme */
  80     int  rw_yylex;       /* token  */
  81 };
  82
  83 rwtable_str rwtable[] = {
  84     "",                 IDENTIFIERTK,
  85     "begin",            BEGINTK,
  86     "end",              ENDTK,
  87     "program",          PROGRAMTK,
  88     "writeln",          WRITETK
  89 };
```

The reserved word table in the code above consists of lexeme strings in alphabetical order and corresponding token values.

```
  Checking Reserved Words (scanner.specs)

  91 #define LEN(x)          (sizeof(x)/sizeof((x)[0]))
  92 #define ENDTABLE(v)     (v - 1 + LEN(v))
  93
  94 int ck_reserved_wd() {
  95         rwtable_str     *low = rwtable;
  96         rwtable_str     *high = ENDTABLE(rwtable);
  97         rwtable_str     *mid;
  98         int comp;
  99         char temp[80];
 100
 101         strcpy(temp,yytext);
 102
 103         while (low <= high)
 104         {       mid = low + (high-low)/2;
 105
 106                 if ((comp=strcmp(mid->rw_name, temp)) == 0)
 107                         return mid->rw_yylex;
 108                 else if (comp < 0)
 109                         low = mid+1;
 110                 else
 111                         high = mid-1;
 112         }
 113         return rwtable->rw_yylex;  /* ie. token: IDENTIFIER! */
 114 }
```

The #define compiler directive specifies the functions *LEN()* and *ENDTABLE()*.
Sizeof() returns the size, in bytes, of an expression or type specifier. The algorithm
used for *ck_reserved_wd()* is a binary search; this over-provision for the example
compiler is obviously preparation for efficient scanning in a full-sized compiler.

The scanner generated by *lex* expects some direction about what it should
do when it encounters an end-of-file. The following listing contains code for the
required function *yywrap()* that instructs the scanner to simply close down at the
first EOF.

```
yywrap() (scanner.fcts)

   1 /*
   2  *        scanner.fcts
   3  */
   4
   5 int yywrap() {
   6         return 1;
   7 }
```

More complex systems might have the scanner open up other files. These instructions would then be placed in *yywrap()*.

6.2.3 Generating the Scanner: Lex

The command

                                lex scanner.specs

converts the information in *scanner.specs* to the file *lex.yy.c* containing C code for
the function *yylex()*. A few of the definitions in this file need to be slightly modified
so that the C++ compiler will accept the code generated by *lex*. In particular,
standard C++ forward references to various functions need to be placed near the
top of the code so that calls to these functions will not be flagged by the compiler.
You can quickly determine the names of the offenders by just compiling the code
and noting the functions that are cited. Also you will want to modify the actual
definitions of two or three functions that cause C++ warnings about old-fashioned C
specification of function arguments. These changes can be easily made by hand, of
course. But they will need to be made every time *lex* is used to generate the scanner.
One way to automate such changes is to use a stream editor to automatically modify
lex.yy.c. The UNIX stream editor *sed* is one such editor. The required modifications
can be easily made by invoking *sed*

                    sed − f scanner.cmd lex.yy.c > scanner.tmp

where *scanner.cmd* is a file of the following *sed* commands.

```
Sed commands (scanner.cmd)

 1 /extern char yytext/i\
 2 #include "scanner.h"
 3 s/p, m)/int *p, int m)/
 4 s/int \*p\;//
 5 s/yyoutput(c)/void yyoutput(int c) {/
 6 s/yyunput(c)/void yyunput(int c) {/
 7 /int c\; {/d
 8 s/yyfussy://
 9 $a\
10 #include "scanner.fcts"
```

The first command (lines 1, 2) places the following collection of "forward references" in *lex.yy.c* immediately after the definition of *yytext*.

```
(scanner.h)

 1 int yylook();
 2 int yyback(int*,int);
 3 void yyless(int);
 4 void yyunput(int);
 5 int yywrap();
 6 void ckout();
 7 int ret_token(int);
 8 int ck_reserved_wd();
```

The commands in lines 3–7 modify the old C style parameter declaration to a form that C++ likes and remove the (now unnecessary) *int p* and *int c* from the file. Since *yyfussy* is never called, its removal quiets a C++ warning. The last file included contains *yywrap()*.

6.3 The Parser: yyparse()

This would be a good time to review Figure 6.1. Recall that the scanner function *yylex()* was produced by *lex* from a scanner specification file. The most important items in that specification file were *regular expressions* and *rules*. The regular expressions defined the set of valid lexemes; the rules specified the actions to be taken by the scanner when lexeme recognition occurs. In much the same way, *yacc* transforms a *parser specification* into a corresponding parsing function *yyparse()*. The most important items in this file are the set of language *tokens* and a set of grammar rules or *productions*.

6.3.1 Parser Specification File

A parser specification file has the following format.

| Header section (optional) |
| Token specification |
| %% |
| Grammar productions |
| %% |
| User-defined supporting functions (optional) |

Header. The Header for the parser specification file is listed below.

```
Parser Specification Header (parser.gram)

1 %{
2 /*
3  *        parser.gram
4  */
5
6 #define YYSTYPE PPTreeNodeCls
7 extern char* textline; //Defined in scanner.specs
8 %}
```

The YYSTYPE in line 6 represents the type of the parser's value stack. This definition specifies that pointers to parse tree nodes are going to be placed on the parser's stack as it recognizes the various parts of a source program. Since the definition of *PTreeNodeCls* does not occur until Chapter 8, you will probably want to comment out this line at this point in the construction of your own compiler.

Line 7 makes reference to a variable that will be used in later stages of compiler development. A copy of the source program text is stored in *textline* so that error messages can display the offending line and indicate possible causes of the error.

Token specification. As noted in Chapter 3, the collection of tokens is determined by the extent of the source language that the compiler will encounter. In our case we are restricting ourselves to the following kinds of source programs.

```
1    program simple;
2    begin
3       j := 3;
4       i := j;
5       writeln(i)
6    end.
```

The following list is one way of breaking the lexemes up into distinct categories.

Token specification (parser.gram)

```
10 %token PROGRAMTK
11 %token BEGINTK
12 %token ENDTK
13 %token SCTK
14 %token ASGTK
15 %token DOTTK
16 %token IDENTIFIERTK
17 %token NUMLITERALTK
18 %token WRITETK
19 %token LPARENTK
20 %token RPARENTK
```

In this case, the lexemes *simple*, *i*, and *j* from the sample program are being placed in the same *IDENTIFIERTK* category. Similarly, any numeric lexeme, such as the *5* will be placed in the *NUMLITERALTK* category.

In this rather trivial example all other lexemes form a one element category. The proportion of such one element categories is usually much smaller, of course.

Productions. The next section of the parser specification file is the listing of the productions. You will possibly recognize these as corresponding roughly to grammars found in most Pascal texts. According to line 22, we are trying to recognize a *Program* that, by line 25, consists of a string of tokens starting with the token corresponding to the reserved word *program*, followed by the token corresponding to a valid Pascal identifier, followed by the token representing the semicolon, and so on.

The C++ code enclosed in braces actually creates a *ProgramCls* object and places its address in *pgm*. The $2 and $4 symbols refer to the second and fourth items on the right side of the production, namely, *Identifier* and *Block*, which will have been recognized earlier and stored for later reference by lines 34 and 67 that use the $$. Details about the definition and implementation of these various parse tree classes are contained in Chapters 8 and 9.

Line 30 indicates that a *Block* consists of the familiar sequence of statements sandwiched between the *begin* and *end*, followed by the famous Pascal "end dot." Note that the example compiler knows only two nontrivial statements (lines 48 and 52). Note further that expressions consist only of numerical literals (lines 60, 70) or the values stored in a variable (lines 62, 65).

```
 Grammar Productions (parser.gram)

 22 %start Program
 23 %%
 24
 25 Program:
 26      PROGRAMTK Identifier SCTK
 27      Block
 28          {PProgramCls pgm = new ProgramCls($2,$4);}
 29      ;
 30 Block:
 31      BEGINTK
 32          StatementSeq
 33      ENDTK DOTTK
 34          {$$ = new BlockCls($2);}
 35      ;
 36 StatementSeq:
 37      Statement
 38          {$$ = new StatementSeqCls($1);}
 39      | StatementSeq SCTK Statement
 40          {$$ = PStatementSeqCls($1) -> append($3);}
 41      ;
 42 Statement:
 43      /* empty */
 44          {$$ = new EmptyStmtCls;}
 45      | AssignmentStmt
 46      | WriteStmt
 47      ;
 48 AssignmentStmt:
 49      Identifier ASGTK Expr
 50          {$$ = new AssignmentStmtCls($1,$3,textline);}
 51      ;
 52 WriteStmt:
 53      WRITETK LPARENTK Expr RPARENTK
 54          {$$ = new WriteStmtCls($3,textline);}
 55      ;
 56 Expr:
 57      Factor
 58      ;
 59 Factor:
 60      Number
 61          {$$ = new NumFactorCls($1);}
 62      | Identifier
 63          {$$ = new VarAccessFactorCls($1);}
 64      ;
 65 Identifier:
 66      IDENTIFIERTK
 67          {$$ = new IdentCls();}
 68      ;
 69 Number:
 70      NUMLITERALTK
 71          {$$ = new NumLiteralCls();}
 72      ;
```

Of special note is the way the grammar deals with a *sequence* of statements. Line 36 indicates that a StatementSeq is either a single Statement (line 37) or a recognized StatementSeq followed by a semicolon followed by a single Statement (line 39). Probably the best way to see how this part of the grammar works is to try it out on several sample statement sequences.

1. Let's first consider the block

```
begin

end.
```

having no statement. No problem; *StatementSeq* can be recognized as a *Statement* (line 37), which can then be recognized as an empty statement (line 43).

2. Next, consider the block

```
begin
    i := 1
end.
```

having a single statement. Again no problem. *StatementSeq* is recognized as a *Statement*, where *Statement* now is an *AssignmentStmt* (line 48).

3. Finally, let's take a block consisting of two statements.

```
begin
    i := 1;
    writeln(i)
end.
```

This time the sequence of two statements is recognized in two steps. Initially the first assignment statement is recognized as a *StatementSeq* just as in the one-statement case. Then both statements as seen as a *StatementSeq*, since they consist of a *StatementSeq* (the *AssignmentStmt*) followed by a semicolon followed by a *Statement* (the output statement). The recognition goes in precisely the same order as the normal program flow of control: from top to bottom. That's an important insight that we will need when we discuss building the parse tree in Chapter 8.

Optional user-supplied functions. The generated parser expects a user-supplied function, *yyerror()*, much the same way the scanner expected *yywrap()*. This function is called whenever the parser encounters a syntax error. The following listing contains rather standard code for such a function.

```
 User-supplied function (parser.fcts)

    1 /*
    2 *        parser.fcts
    3 */
    4
    5 #include <stream.h>
    6 void yyerror(char* s) {
    7         cout << "error has occurred..." << s << endl;
    8 }
```

Placing this kind of code in the grammar specification file can be somewhat ineffi-
cient. Any modifications made to these functions require generating the complete
parser. An alternative plan is to place them in a separate file that is either included
by some implementation module or compiled separately.

6.3.2   Generating the Parser: Yacc

The command

$$yacc \ -vd \ parser.gram$$

produces a file[2] $y.tab.c$ containing C code for the function $yyparse()$.

As was the case for the scanner, a few of the constructions in this file need to be
slightly modified so that the C++ compiler will also accept this code. Early forward
referencing of function names and minor modifications to the C definitions of a few
functions can be performed by sed

$$sed - f \ parser.cmd \ \ y.tab.c > parser.tmp$$

to place a modified copy of the normal parser $y.tab.c$ into our file $parser.tmp$.

```
 String Editor Commands (parser.cmd)

    1 /define YYERRCODE/a\
    2 #include "parser.h"
    3 /yynewerror:/d
    4 /yyerrlab:/d
    5 /++yynerrs;/d
    6 $a\
    7 #include "parser.fcts"
```

$Parser.h$ just contains the two forward referencing commands, **int yylex();** and
void yyerror(char*);

---

[2] Recall that the -d option produces the file $y.tab.h$ of token definitions. The -v option produces
the file $y.output$, that is useful for debugging or modifying the parser.

6.4   Module Makefile

The *ScanparseCls Makefile* does give some indication of *make*'s flexibility.

```
scanparse/Makefile

  1    #Makefile for Pascal Compiler parser
  2    PROGRAM:        scanparse.o
  3
  4    scanparse.o:    ../p_tree/p_tree.h scanparse.h scanparse.C\
  5                    scanparse.fct
  6                    CC -c -g scanparse.C
  7
  8    scanparse.fct:  parser.tmp scanner.tmp
  9                    cat scanner.tmp parser.tmp > scanparse.fct
 10
 11    scanner.tmp:    scanner.h scanner.specs scanner.fcts parser.gram
 12                    lex scanner.specs
 13                    sed -f scanner.cmd lex.yy.c > scanner.tmp
 14                    rm lex.yy.c
 15
 16    parser.tmp:     parser.h parser.gram parser.fcts
 17                    byacc -vd parser.gram
 18                    sed -f parser.cmd y.tab.c > parser.tmp
 19                    rm y.tab.c
 20
 21    clean:
 22                    rm -f *.o lex.yy.c y.tab.c y.o* *tmp*\
 23                    scanparse.fct y.tab.h a.out
 24
 25    print:
 26                    /usr/5bin/pr -n scanparse.h scanparse.C\
 27                    scanner.specs parser.gram Makefile > Scanparse.lst
 28                    a2ps Scanparse.lst | lpr -Pmlw
 29                    rm -f Scanparse.lst
 30
 31    count:
 32                    wc *.cmd *.fcts *.specs *.gram *.h *.C Makefile
```

What *make* actually does is to create *scanner.tmp* and *parser.tmp*[3] and then cate-
nate the two files storing the result in *scanparse.fct* in lines 8 and 9.

6.5   Summary

The following items have been described in this chapter.

- Review of important terms: lexeme, token, scanner, and parser.

- LexTokCls for scanner-parser communication.

---

[3]Lines 12 and 17 are using *lex* and *yacc* as described in Sections 6.1, 6.2, and 6.3. Lines 13 and
18 call the UNIX stream editor *sed* to massage the files *lex.yy.c* and *y.tab.c* into forms that most
C++ compilers can tolerate.

- ScanparseCls definition and implementation.

- Process for building the scanner.

- Process for building the parser.

- Makefile for the scanner, parser and the encapsulating *ScanparseCls*.

6.6 Suggested Activities

1. (a) Write C++ code defining your own version of *ScanparseCls*.

   (b) Write C++ code implementing your version of *ScanparseCls*.
       Suggestion: Comment out references to files or objects not yet created.

   (c) Test the entire system at its present level of development. Note your
       progress on the system development schedule in Figure 3.3.

2. Construct a simple scanner for your project. You may find the following steps
   helpful.

   (a) Create a very simple parser specification file, say, *parser.gram*, containing
       the set of tokens you will need for your compiler. The following is an
       example of a trivial parser specification file.

```
 ┌──────────────────────────┐
 │ Minimal Pascal Grammar   │
 ├──────────────────────────┘
 %token FIRST
 %Token SECOND

 %start Program
 %%
 Program:
      ;
```

   (b) Create the corresponding set *y.tab.h* of token definitions, using the $-d$
       option illustrated in the following command.

$$\text{yacc } -d \text{ parser.gram}$$

   (c) Create a scanner specification file.
       Suggestion: Make all the scanner actions simple output statements.

   (d) Build and test the scanner as follows.
       i. Use *lex* to produce the function *yylex()*.
       ii. Write a *main()* that calls *yylex()* until a zero is returned, indicating
           the end of the input stream.
       iii. Write a simple function *yywrap()* as illustrated in this chapter.

   (e) i. Compile and link your program with the C compiler:

     A. Compile the main program: `cc -c main.c`

     B. Compile the scanner: `cc -c lex.yy.c`

     C. Compile the wrap-up function: `cc -c yywrap.c`

     D. Link: `cc main.o lex.yy.o yywrap.o`

  ii. Test the program on several sample character streams. Recall that *yylex()* is expecting input from *stdin*.

(f) Let's see what happens when we use C++ instead of C.

  i. Compile lex.yy.c using the command `CC -c lex.yy.c`. Note and correct the following kinds of problems.

- If your output statements use *printf*, you may need to include the system file *stdio.h*.

- Message: "lex.yy.c", line 32: error: undefined function yylook called.
  Look at the definition of *yylook* in *lex.yy.c* and at the locations where it is called. Determine the return type (if any), and then make a forward reference like

$$\texttt{void yylook()}$$

or

$$\texttt{int yylook()}$$

at some place in *lex.yy.c* prior to the offending call.

- Message: "lex.yy.c", line 37: error: undefined function yywrap called.
  Place an "extern int yywrap()" declaration in *lex.yy.c*.
  Question: Why did this message show up only under compilation by C++ ?

- Message: "lex.yy.c", line 262: warning: old style definition of yyback().
  Note that a C function header of the form

```
yyback(p, m)
        int *p;
        {
```
should be changed to the corresponding C++ version
```
int yyback(int *p, int m)
        {
```
in order to quiet such warnings.

3. Construct a simple parser for your project. You may find the following steps helpful.

(a) Modify the parser specification file from Activity 2.

(b) Make a separate file containing *main()* and remove *main()* from the scanner specification file. This main just needs to make a single call to *yyparse()*.

(c) Separately compile the scanner, parser and main. Link the files and test the system.

4. **#Include** the simple scanner and parser from Activities 2 and 3 in the implementation module for *ScanparseCls*.

5. Now, let's flesh-out a "complete" scanparse module for your project.

(a) Automate making the changes to *lex.yy.c* using *sed* or your own favorite utility.

(b) Automate making the changes to *y.tab.c* using *sed* or your own favorite utility.

(c) Place whatever commands are necessary in the makefile for the scanparse module.

(d) Modify the parser specification file to include all the tokens you will be using.

(e) Modify the scanner specification file to return the new tokens.

(f) Modify the parser specification file to include the desired new productions.

(g) If necessary, modify the *Scanparse.C* so that the new versions of the scanner and parser are included into the module. Compile the module.

(h) Test your scanparse module.

- Use a program having no statements.
- Use a program having a single assignment statement. Try "terminating" the statement with a semicolon. Can you explain the parser's behavior?
- Use the program indicated in Activity 9.

6. (a) Extend your scanner specification file so that it also includes a regular expression that will recognize a valid Pascal real literal.

(b) Test your scanner on various correct and incorrect versions of real literals.

7. (a) Extend your scanner specification file so that it includes a regular expression that recognizes a valid Pascal string literal.

(b) Test your scanner on various correct and incorrect versions of string literals.

8. Extend your scanner/parser system to allow for the recognition of a selection statement.

   Suggestion: No selection statement is trivial to recognize; perhaps the best one to try is the usual Pascal *if*. You may want to consult a Pascal grammar (see [4], [5] or [13]) for ideas on incorporating the six relational operators $<$, $<=$, ... into the normal expression productions.

   (a) Add the required new tokens to the parser specification file.

   (b) Modify your scanner specification file to return these new tokens.

   (c) Add the required productions to allow for the recognition of a selection statement.

   (d) Test your expanded compiler on a source program that includes a selection statement that is valid for your syntax rule.

9. Trace through the productions that are used to recognize the following program.

```
program trace;
begin
    i := 1;
    j := i;
    writeln(i);
end.
```

Chapter 7

Symbol Table Module

A compiler uses a symbol table the way we use dictionaries or encyclopedias. When we need more information about a word we look up the word and then find the information stored in a rather standard format. When a compiler needs additional information about any identifier, the compiler performs a *lookup()* of the identifier and finds the information in the form of a *SymtabEntryCls* object.

Dictionaries are reference books or computer files containing words alphabetically arranged along with information about their forms, pronunciation, historical development and meanings. Symbol tables are *objects* that contain identifiers arranged according to order of encounter along with information about the identifier's purpose, location in the source program, values, etc. In compiler literature, the term **identifier** is most often replaced by *name*; the identifier's *information items* are called **attributes**.

7.1 Symbol Table Module Header

```
Symtab header (symtab.C)

4 #include <iostream.h>
5 #include <string.h>
6
7 #include "symtab.h"
8 /* end-header */
```

7.2 ScopeCls

Most compilers use a number of symbol tables to provide information about the **scope** or location in the original source program in which a particular variable can be seen. An elementary version of *ScopeCls* is therefore appropriate for this compiler.

```
 ScopeCls Definition (symtab.h)

   9 typedef class ScopeCls *PScopeCls;
  10 class ScopeCls {
  11    public:
  12        ScopeCls()                {;}
  13        static SymtabCls      *get_vista() {return vista;}
  14        friend class ControllerCls;
  15    private:
  16        static SymtabCls      *vista;
  17 };
```

It consists of a trivial constructor, a static function *get_vista()*, and a static member *vista* that points to the current symbol table. Static functions and members belong to classes rather than objects: *ScopeCls :: get_vista()* returns the value of the symbol table presently visible, without having to first construct a *ScopeCls* object. *ControllerCls* is a *friend* so that it can set the initial value of *vista* to the original symbol table.[1]

7.3   SymtabEntryCls

Symbol tables are just arrays of *SymtabEntryCls* objects, arranged in such a way that table entries and lookups are relatively efficient. Since all symbol table entries must be associated with some identifier, the *SymtabEntryCls* constructor defined below requires a string-valued *Name* argument, which is then stored in the corresponding class member *name*.

The elementary compiler allows only one kind of identifier: the name of a variable. There will therefore be only one subclass of *SymtabEntryCls*, and it needs to store the relevant values or *attributes* associated with a Pascal variable. Since all variables are required to be of integer type, the *VarAttCls* therefore need only store the (integer) *value* of that variable.

The implementation details for *SymtabEntryCls()* and *VarAttCls()* are routine and are left for you to complete.

---

[1] *Some* object needs to initialize *vista*, since constructors are rarely used for classes with mostly static members.

```
┌────────────────────────────────────────────────────────────────┐
│  ┌─────────────────────────────────────────┐                    │
│  │ SymtabEntryCls Definition (symtab.h) │                       │
│  └─────────────────────────────────────────┘                    │
│                                                                  │
│  19 typedef class SymtabEntryCls *PSymtabEntryCls;               │
│  20 class SymtabEntryCls   {                                     │
│  21    public:                                                   │
│  22         SymtabEntryCls() {;}                                 │
│  23         SymtabEntryCls(char *Name);                          │
│  24         friend class    SymtabCls;                           │
│  25         virtual int     emit();                              │
│  26    protected:                                                │
│  27         char            *name;                               │
│  28 };                                                           │
│  29                                                              │
│  30 typedef class VarAttCls *PVarAttCls;                         │
│  31 class VarAttCls : public SymtabEntryCls {                    │
│  32    public:                                                   │
│  33         VarAttCls()      {;}                                 │
│  34         VarAttCls(char* Name, int Value);                    │
│  35         void            set_value(int Value);                │
│  36         int             get_value()                          │
│  37                              {return value;}                 │
│  38         int             emit();                              │
│  39    private:                                                  │
│  40         int value;                                           │
│  41 };                                                           │
└────────────────────────────────────────────────────────────────┘
```

7.4 SymtabCls

The class abstracting the notion of an entire symbol table is *SymtabCls*.

```
┌────────────────────────────────────────────────────────────────┐
│  ┌─────────────────────────────────────────┐                    │
│  │ SymtabCls Definition (symtab.h) │                            │
│  └─────────────────────────────────────────┘                    │
│                                                                  │
│  52 typedef class SymtabCls *PSymtabCls;                         │
│  53 class SymtabCls   {                                          │
│  54    public:                                                   │
│  55         SymtabCls();                                         │
│  56         int             insert(PSymtabEntryCls);             │
│  57         PSymtabEntryCls lookup(char*);                       │
│  58         int             emit();                              │
│  59    private:                                                  │
│  60         int             tablesize;                           │
│  61         int             next_location;                       │
│  62         int             *hashtable;                          │
│  63         PSymtabEntryCls *symtab;  //N.B.:  pointers!         │
│  64         int             hash(char *);                        │
│  65 };                                                           │
└────────────────────────────────────────────────────────────────┘
```

In addition to the expected constructors and the member functions *insert()* and
lookup(), the class definition for *SymtabCls* contains a number of private members
that may need some explanation.

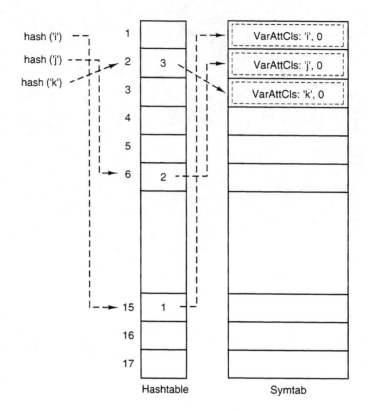

Figure 7.1. Symbol Table Configuration (Attempt 1)

Mature versions of object-oriented symbol tables exhibit an interesting growing phenomenon. Small tables are more efficient than huge ones; compiler writers cannot predict maximum size requirements prior to compilation time, so tables are initialized at a smaller size and then allowed to grow if the extra size is needed. Tables in this simple compiler don't have the growing capability, but they do contain the variable member *tablesize* in anticipation of this feature.

The member *next_location* is just a convenience variable containing the index of the next open location in the symbol table. It is used primarily for deciding where to store the next *SymtabEntryCls* object and for keeping count of the number of active table entries.

The next three private *SymtabCls* members, *hashtable*, *symtab*, and *hash()*, are slightly involved. Lookups in a table are just searches through an array. One way to make such searches more efficient is to use a hashing algorithm. Since it is often important to retain the order in which the various identifiers have been encountered in the source program, symbol tables are often made of two arrays, much like those illustrated in Figure 7.1. Symbol table entries are entered sequentially into the

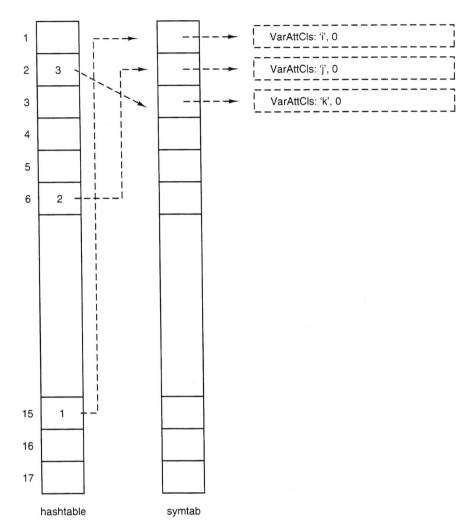

Figure 7.2. Symbol Table Configuration (Attempt 2)

array *symtab* on the right; the appropriate entry of *hasharray* on the left is just adjusted to point to the corresponding entry of *symtab*. Unfortunately[2] C++ does not allow efficient assignment of complex class structures. The array of symbol table entries must therefore be replaced by an array of *pointers* to symbol table entries as illustrated in Figure 7.2.

---

[2] Actually, *fortunately*, as later work will show!

```
  SymtabCls Constructor (symtab.C)

  41 SymtabCls :: SymtabCls() {
  42     //cout << "SymtabCls::()"<< endl;
  43     tablesize = 17;     //Must be a prime for good performance
  44     hashtable = new int[tablesize];
  45     next_location = 1;  // sacrifice 0th spot - hashtable empty:NIL
  46     symtab = new PSymtabEntryCls[tablesize]; // Note "P" !!!!
  47     PSymtabEntryCls tmp = new SymtabEntryCls("    ");
  48     for (int i=0; i<tablesize; i++) {
  49         hashtable[i] = 0;
  50         symtab[i] = tmp;
  51     }
  52 }
```

The particular hashing algorithm used in this compiler is from Aho's dragon book [2] where it is attributed to P. J. Weinberger's C compiler. Its only requirement is that the size of the table be a prime. Seventeen seems like a good prime for a tiny compiler. Line 46 declares *symtab* to be an array of pointers that is initialized in the loop found at lines 48–51.

```
  SymtabCls :: hash() (symtab.C)

  54 int SymtabCls :: hash(char *s) {
  55     //cout << "SymtabCls :: hashing for " << s ;
  56     char* ss = s;
  57     unsigned int h = 0, g;
  58     for (; *ss != '\0'; ss++) {
  59         h = (h << 4) + *ss;
  60         if (g = h & 0xf0000000) {
  61             h ^= g >> 24;        // fold top 4 bits onto ------X-
  62             h ^= g;              // clear top 4 bits
  63         }
  64     }
  65     //cout << "hashing to " << h % tablesize << endl;
  66     return h % tablesize ;
  67 }
```

Aho cites interesting performance information indicating that the algorithm is fast and has relatively few collisions.

The code for *SymtabCls::insert()* comes next.

```
      SymtabCls :: insert() (symtab.C)

   69 int SymtabCls :: insert(PSymtabEntryCls info) {
   70      //cout << "SymtabCls::insert()" << endl;
   71      //Return 0 if insert successful; else location in symtab.
   72
   73      //Look for open slot in the hashtable....
   74      int Try, hash_try; //'try' can be a reserved word
   75      char *Name = info -> name;
   76      //cout<<"preparing to enter"<<Name<<"\n";
   77      Try = hash(Name);
   78      //cout << "preparing to go into hash table at " << Try << endl;
   79
   80      while (hash_try = hashtable[Try]) { //something's in hashtable
   81          //Check to see if it's the same thing we want to insert...
   82          if (!strcmp((symtab[hash_try] -> name), Name)) {
   83              return hash_try; //it's already there!
   84          } else if (++Try >= tablesize) {
   85              //resolve collision by looking for open spot ...
   86              Try = 0; //wrap around
   87          }
   88          //Mature (growing) tables can be at most 2/3 full,
   89      }
   90      // So an open spot MUST be found
   91      hashtable[Try] = next_location;
   92      //cout << "entered current loc'n in table " << Try << endl;
   93      symtab[next_location++] = info; //Since they're both pointers
   94      return 0; // success!
   95 }
```

The identifier, stored in *Name* is hashed into the table at the location stored in *Try* (line 77). *Hash_try* is *assigned* the value of the *hashtable* at *Try*. As long as it is nonzero, compare the symbol table entry's identifier with the *Name* being inserted (lines 80–90). If the *Name* is already there, exit from the function; otherwise, increment *Try*, checking and looking for an open location. Notice that *Try* may wrap around to the top of the array if necessary. Line 93 is one of the main reasons for making the *symtab* an array of pointers: efficiency of assignment. Some of the scaffolding used in the program development has been left in the code with the hope that you will find similar code instructive as you build and test your own symbol tables.

It is an interesting exercise to trace *insert()*'s behavior when the table gets full. A more mature version of *insert()* would test the number of entries after each successful insertion and create a larger symbol table when the present table had reached some critical size. Empirical data and theoretical analyses both indicate that hashing collisions begin to occur sufficiently often to justify the work of re-creating the table when the table becomes approximately two-thirds full.

Lookup() is our final symbol table function. The argument to *lookup()* is a string, since lookups can only be made on identifiers.

```
SymtabCls :: lookup() (symtab.C)

 97 PSymtabEntryCls SymtabCls :: lookup(char *Name) {
 98     //cout << "SymtabCls :: lookup for " << Name ;
 99     int cur_table_size = tablesize;
100     int try, orig_try, hash_try;
101
102     orig_try = try = hash(Name);
103 //cout << "orig_try " << orig_try << "\n";
104     hash_try = hashtable[try];
105 //cout << "hash_try " << hash_try << endl;
106     while (hash_try) {
107         if (!strcmp(symtab[hash_try] -> name, Name)) {
108             return symtab[hash_try];
109         }
110         if (++try >= cur_table_size) try = 0; // wrap around
111         if (try == orig_try) {
112             return symtab[0];
113         } else {
114             hash_try = hashtable[try];
115         }
116 //cout << "hash_try " << hash_try << endl;
117     }
118         return 0; //Failure!
119 }
```

7.5   Module Makefile

The following makefile just issues the C++ command for compiling the implementation file *symtab.C*.

```
symtab/Makefile

 1 # Makefile for symtab
 2 PROGRAM: symtab.o
 3
 4 symtab.o:       symtab.h symtab.C
 5         CC -c -g symtab.C
 6
 7 clean:
 8         rm -f *.o a.out
 9
10 print:
11         /usr/5bin/pr -n symtab.h symtab.C Makefile > Symtab.lst
12         a2ps Symtab.lst | lpr -Pmlw
13         rm -f Symtab.lst
14
15 count:
16         wc *.h *.C Makefile
```

7.6 Summary

We have discussed definition and/or implementation details for the following classes.

- **ScopeCls**

  Scope is the portion of the source program in which an identifier has meaning. **Vista** is the collection of all identifiers that can be accessed at a particular location in the source program.

- **SymtabEntryCls** and **VarAttCls**

  Symbol tables are essentially arrays of *SymtabEntryCls* objects. Identifiers in the elementary compiler can represent only variables and those can be only of type integer. The symbol table entries for these identifiers are of class *VarAttCls*.

- **SymtabCls** Searching sequentially through an array for an identifier is not efficient once the table is reasonably large. *SymtabCls* encapsulates the data and function members for implementing reasonably fast storage and retrieval of identifier information.

7.7 Suggested Activities

1. Write the implementation code for *SymtabEntryCls()* and *VarAttCls()*.

2. Weinberger's algorithm is a very remarkable hashing function.

   (a) Describe this algorithm by carefully explaining:
       i. The loop in line 58.
       ii. The shift and masking in lines 59 and 60.
       iii. The folding in lines 61 and 62.
       iv. How the algorithm deals with strings of length greater than one.

   (b) i. Write a program that tests Weinberger's algorithm on each of the (upper- and lower-case) alphabetical characters. You may want to adjust the value of *tablesize*.
       ii. Describe the distribution of the various hashing values from your sample run above.
       iii. Describe the number of collisions that would have occurred for the various table sizes.

   (c) Test the algorithm an a larger selection of strings.

Chapter 8

Parse Tree Nodes

This chapter describes the class definitions for the various parse tree nodes used by the example compiler. The parse tree is probably the single most important compiler structure. It is produced by the parser during the scanning/parsing phase.

When the entire right-hand side of a grammar rule has been recognized, the parse tree node representing the left-hand side will be created and stored on the parser's value stack.

8.1 An Example

Before we can specify the definition details of each parse tree node, we really need to know the process by which the parser constructs the tree.

Let's trace the parser's action on the following program.

```
1   program Simple;
2   begin
3       i := 1;
4       writeln(i)
5   end.
```

You will probably want to use the grammar from Chapter 6, and also reproduced on page 76, as you trace through the steps. The scanner will translate the above program into the following sequence of tokens.

```
PROGRAMTK, IDENTIFIERTK, SCTK, BEGINTK, IDENTIFIERTK,
ASGTK, NUMLITERALTK, SCTK, WRITETK, LPARENTK,
IDENTIFIER, RPARENTK, ENDTK, DOTTK
```

```
22 %start Program
23 %%
24
25 Program:
26     PROGRAMTK Identifier SCTK
27     Block
28         {PProgramCls pgm = new ProgramCls($2,$4);}
29     ;
30 Block:
31     BEGINTK
32         StatementSeq
33     ENDTK DOTTK
34         {$$ = new BlockCls($2);}
35     ;
36 StatementSeq:
37     Statement
38         {$$ = new StatementSeqCls($1);}
39     | StatementSeq SCTK Statement
40         {$$ = PStatementSeqCls($1) -> append($3);}
41     ;
42 Statement:
43     /* empty */
44         {$$ = new EmptyStmtCls;}
45     | AssignmentStmt
46     | WriteStmt
47     ;
48 AssignmentStmt:
49     Identifier ASGTK Expr
50         {$$ = new AssignmentStmtCls($1,$3,textline);}
51     ;
52 WriteStmt:
53     WRITETK LPARENTK Expr RPARENTK
54         {$$ = new WriteStmtCls($3,textline);}
55     ;
56 Expr:
57     Factor
58     ;
59 Factor:
60     Number
61         {$$ = new NumFactorCls($1);}
62     | Identifier
63         {$$ = new VarAccessFactorCls($1);}
64     ;
65 Identifier:
66     IDENTIFIERTK
67         {$$ = new IdentCls();}
68     ;
69 Number:
70     NUMLITERALTK
71         {$$ = new NumLiteralCls();}
72     ;
```

It is helpful to imagine these tokens as values along a vertical axis and visualize them as causing the parser to use certain productions and take certain actions as illustrated in Figures 8.1 and 8.2.

The parser is in the business of accepting or rejecting the tokens in this sequence. Of course, this activity must be based upon the grammar productions that contain either the tokens or nonterminals that represent a subsequence of the tokens.

First, note that the production

(25) *Program* : *PROGRAMTK@ Identifier SCKT Block*

is expecting the first token PROGRAMTK in the sequence.[1] In order to recognize the second token we place the first production on hold and switch to the following production.

(65) *Identifier* : *IDENTIFIERTK@*

In this case the entire right side of the production has been completed. The grammar instruction

$$\{\$\$ = new IdentCls; \}$$

following the production, called a **parser action** is then executed. Here, an *IdentCls* object is **instantiated**[2] and its address is placed on the parser **value stack**, denoted by $\$\$$, for later use by the waiting parser action from production 25.[3] Thus far the entire parse tree consists of a single *IdentCls* object node representing the identifier *Simple*.

Since production 65 has been completed, or as we say **reduced**, we return to production 25 where we are able to recognize SCTK.

(25) *Program* : *PROGRAMTK Identifier SCKT@ Block*

The next item in the production is the nonterminal *Block*, whose production

(30) *Block* : *BEGINTK@ StatementSeqENDTKDOTTK*

can be used to recognize BEGINTK.

Now we begin an interesting parsing stage (see Figure 8.1). *StatementSeq*, the next item in production 30 is first recognized as a *Statement* and then as an *AssignmentStmt* whose production

(48) *AssignmentStmt* : *Identifier ASGTK Expr*

is expecting an *Identifier*. The reduction of production 65 will again create an *IdentCls* object, this time for the identifier *i*, allowing recognition of the subsequent token ASGTK.

(48) *AssignmentStmt* : *Identifier ASGTK@ Expr*

---

[1] The symbol @ is used to indicate the progress of the recognition process.

[2] The C++ **new** instruction **instantiates** objects, i.e., It: (1) Allocates space on the free store, (2) Calls the class constructor to initialize the object, and (3) Returns the object's address.

[3] "Production *nn*" where *nn* is a grammar line number is just an abbreviated way of saying "the grammar production that starts at line *nn*" on page 76.

Token	Current Production	Waiting List	Parse Tree
PROGRAMTK	25)Program: PROGRAMTK @Identifier SCTK Block		
IDENTIFIERTK	65)Identifier: IDENTIFIERTK @ {$$ = new IdentCls;}	25	Simple
	25)Program: PROGRAMTK Identifier@ SCTK Block		
SCTK	25)Program: PROGRAMTK Identifier SCTK @ Block		
BEGINTK	30)Block: BEGINTK @ StatementSeq ENDTK DOTTK		
IDENTIFIERTK	36)StatementSeq: @ Statement	30,25	
	42)Statement: @ AssignmentSmt	36,30,25	
	48)AssignmentStmt: @Identifier ASGTK Expr	42,36,30,25	
	65)Identifier: IDENTIFIERTK @ {$$ = new IdentCls;}	48,42,36,30,25	
	48)AssignmentStmt: Identifier @ ASGTK Expr		
ASGTK	48)AssignmentStmt: Identifier ASGTK@ Expr		
NUMLITRLTK	56)Expr: @Factor	48,42,36,30,25	
	59)Factor: @ Number	56,48,42,36,30,25	
	70)Number: NUMLITRLTK@ {$$ = new NumLiteralCls;}	59,56,48,42,36,30,25	
	59)Factor: Number @ {$$ = new NumFactorCls($1);}		
	56)Expr: Factor@		
	48)AssignmentStmt: Identifier ASGTK Expr@ {$$ = new AssignmentStmt($1,$3);}		
	42)Statement: AssignmentSmt@		
	36)StatementSeq: Statement@ {$$ = new StatementSeqCls($1);}		
SCTK	36)StatementSeq: StatementSeq SCTK @ Statement		
WRITETK	40)Statement: @WriteStmt	36,30,25	
	52)WriteStmt: WRITETK @ LPAREN Identifier RPARENTK	40,36,30,25	
LPARENTK	52)WriteStmt: WRITETK LPAREN @ Identifier RPARENTK		
IDENTIFIERTK	56)Expr: @ Factor	52,40,36,30,25	
	59)Factor: @Identifier	56,52,40,36,30,25	
	65)Identifier: IDENTIFIERTK @ {$$ = new IdentCls;}	59,56,52,40,36,30,25	
	59)Factor: Identifier @ {$$ = new VarAccessFactorCls;}		

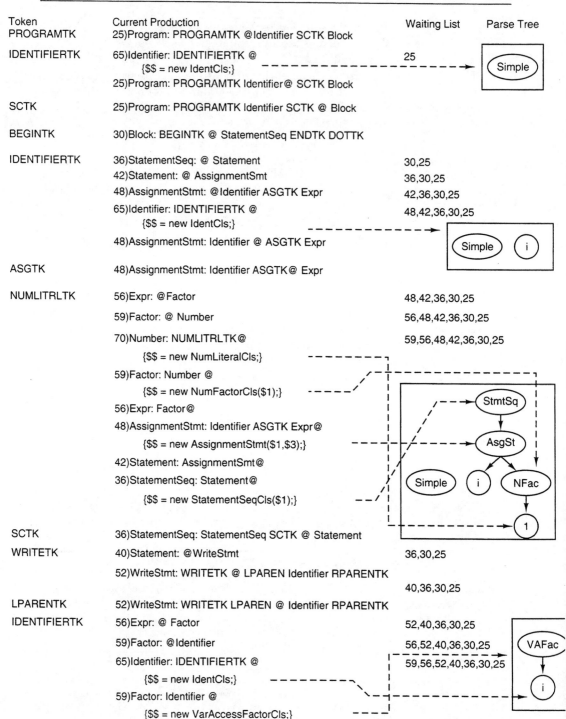

Figure 8.1. Building the Parse Tree (Part 1)

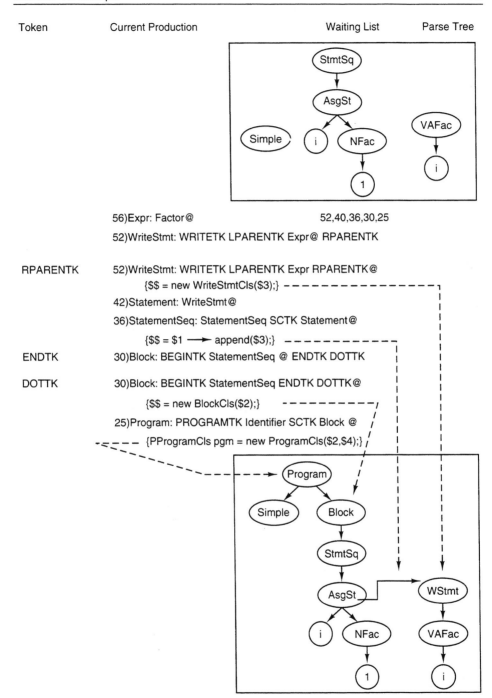

Token   Current Production   Waiting List   Parse Tree

56)Expr: Factor@   52,40,36,30,25

52)WriteStmt: WRITETK LPARENTK Expr@ RPARENTK

RPARENTK   52)WriteStmt: WRITETK LPARENTK Expr RPARENTK@
            {$$ = new WriteStmtCls($3);}
            42)Statement: WriteStmt@
            36)StatementSeq: StatementSeq SCTK Statement@
            {$$ = $1 ⟶ append($3);}
ENDTK   30)Block: BEGINTK StatementSeq @ ENDTK DOTTK

DOTTK   30)Block: BEGINTK StatementSeq ENDTK DOTTK@
            {$$ = new BlockCls($2);}
            25)Program: PROGRAMTK Identifier SCTK Block @
            {PProgramCls pgm = new ProgramCls($2,$4);}

Figure 8.2. Building the Parse Tree (Part 2)

It remains to recognize the next token NUMLITERALTK as an *Expr*. An *Expr* is a *Factor* (production 56) and *Factor*s are by 59 *Number*s.

$$(69) \ Number: NUMLITERALTK@$$

Since this production is now reduced, the parser action

$$\{\$\$ = newNumLiteralCls; \}$$

then instantiates an object representing the numeric value. The tree now consists of three separate nodes. But then production 59

$$(59) \ Factor: Number@$$

has been completely reduced so that the action

$$\{\$\$ = newNumFactorCls(\$1); \}$$

creates a *NumFactorCls* object pointing to the NumLiteralCls node previously placed on the parser's value stack.[4] Since this completely reduces production 48, an *AssignmentCls* object is instantiated, pointing to the identifier and numeric factor tree nodes. Similarly productions 42 and then 36 have now been reduced, so a *StatementSeq* object is created and made to point to the assignment tree node.

Note well how the parse tree in the example is built.

- Parse tree nodes are produced by a parser action when a production is completely reduced.

- Parser actions create parse tree nodes by using the C++ *new* operator and then place the address of the created node on the parser's value stack.

- Object-oriented parse trees are most easily formed from the bottom up. Leaves are produced first, then parents and then higher level ancestors.

The remainder of the token recognition steps in Figures 8.1 and 8.2 are rather routine except for one important construct: the recognition of the sequence of the two statements in the source program. After the assignment statement has been accepted as a statement sequence, the next token SCTK gives the parser a clue that the end of the block has not yet been reached. So instead of looking for ENDTK and DOTTK, the parser again considers production 36 (Figure 8.2), but this time the recursive version

$$(36) \ StatementSeq: \ StatementSeq \ SCTK@ \ Statement$$

---

[4] The notation $k is used to reference any item stored on the parser's value stack when the *k*th item on the right hand side of the production was recognized.

is used. The subsequent string of tokens received by the parser lead to the recognition of the *writeln(i)* as a statement and so this version of production 36 is reduced and its parser action

$$\{ \; \$\$ = \$1 \; \rightarrow \; append(\$3); \; \} \tag{8.1}$$

is called. This action directs the *StatementSeqCls* object, *$1*, previously constructed in Figure 8.1, to *append()* *$3*, the *WriteStmtCls* object. If there were more statements in this block, the same production would be used to append the parse tree nodes for those statements to this linked list of statements.

When the tree is completed, it will look like the one in the diagram at the bottom right corner of Figure 8.2, not exactly a beautiful, balanced binary tree, but a tree nonetheless and a very useful one at that!

8.2 Description of Module

In the sections below, we systematically examine the various classes used in the definition of parse tree nodes. One of the indications of the importance of the parse tree is the size of the corresponding module (Figure 8.3). In addition to a definition file *p_tree.h* and a class-oriented[5] file *p_tree.C*, there are two function-oriented[6] files *interp.C* (discussed in Chapter 10) and *emit.C* (Chapter 11).

The class definition strategy used in the sections below will be to first construct a module-wide base class, then to define the various leaves of the parse tree, and then move to successively higher level tree nodes.

8.3 PTreeNodeCls: The Base Class

This class serves several important roles in the construction of the parser and the design of the parse tree. The discussion surrounding the construction of the parse tree in Figures 8.1 and 8.2 clearly illustrates that the parser stores the addresses of the newly created parse tree nodes on a value stack symbolized by $$. Since all the different kinds of nodes must be placed on this stack, it is a great savings of effort to be able to type the value stack as a pointer to *PTreeNodeCls* rather than a complex union or variant field structure.

PTreeNodeCls also contains the one attribute and useful member functions that occur in (most of) the parse tree classes. *PTreeNodeCls* is therefore called a **base class** for all parse tree node classes. In this case we say that these nodes are **derived** from *PTreeNodeCls* and that they **inherit** the functionalities of *PTreeNodeCls*.

PTreeNodeCls: definition. In the example compiler, the only attribute common to the various parse tree nodes is that of the underlying lexeme represented by the

---

[5] An implementation file is said to be **class-oriented** if it contains the usual class constructors and member functions arranged in class order.

[6] An implementation file is **function-oriented** if it contains the implementation details of the same function for a collection of classes.

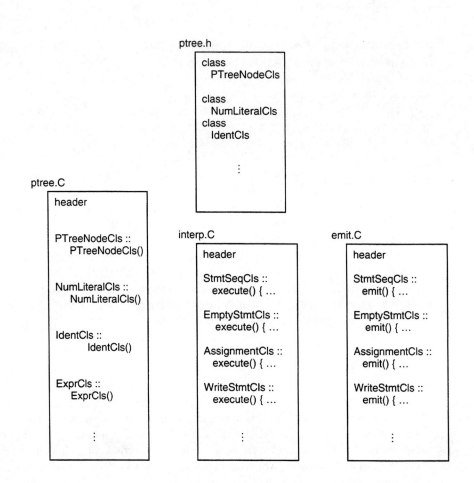

Figure 8.3. Parse Tree Module

parse tree object. So the only data member in the definition of *PTreeNodeCls* is
the pointer *lt* to the current *LexTokCls* object (Section 6.1.2).

```
PTreeNodeCls Definition (p_tree.h)

19  typedef class PTreeNodeCls *PPTreeNodeCls;
20  class PTreeNodeCls {
21    public:
22          PTreeNodeCls();
23          virtual int        emit();
24          virtual int        execute();
25          virtual void       print();
26          virtual LexTokCls  *get_lex_tok()
27                                    {return lt;}
28    protected:
29          LexTokCls          *lt;
30  };
```

The member functions are a different story, a story involving **dynamic** or **late
binding**. Suppose you need to produce an interpreter for your compiling system.
The traditional approach would be to construct a giant interpreter and pass the
parse tree to the interpreter as parameter fodder. The interpreter would traverse
the tree and then determine appropriate behavior based upon the nature of each
node. Normal recursive tree traversal techniques are often not directly applicable,
since the parse tree form can be so variable and unpredictable. Such interpreters are
often coded as complex selection structures. Data structures are usually complex
record structures, many containing extensive variant fields.

The object-oriented approach is the other way around. Build into each tree
node the ability to *execute()* that part of the program it understands best: itself!
The *ProgramCls* object simply tells its *BlockCls* member to *execute()*; *BlockCls*
tells *StatementSeqCls* to *execute()*; *StatementSeqCls* tells each of the statements
in its linked list to *execute()* and there we have it—an interpreter! Instead of every
parse tree node having a separately named *execute()* function as would be required
in a procedurally oriented language, we will call all the functions by the same name.
And because the definition of *execute()* for the base class has been declared **virtual**
for the *PTreeNodeCls* base class, the selection of the specific version of *execute()* will
be determined at *runtime*, based upon the nature of the object receiving the execute
message! *StatementSeqCls* doesn't know what kind of statements are down there
in that linked list. It doesn't need to know! It just says: Each of you objects down
that list, *execute()*. Then, based on the identity of the various objects in that list,
the correct *execute()* function is selected and performed at runtime: **late binding**.
No giant interpreter, just many small, cooperating *execute()*s quietly doing their
job. Implementation details of the various *execute()* functions are found in the
interp submodule described in Chapter 10.

Exactly the same kind of thing can also be done with generating code: Each
parse tree node will be given an *emit()* behavior. The root of the parse tree will
then be requested to emit, and so on. Details about the code generator functions

are found in the emitter submodule described in Chapter 11.

8.4   NumLiteralCls

Having completed the definition of the base class *PTreeNodeCls*, we now move to
our first **leaf class**. This example compiler recognizes only integral valued literals.
The parse tree class that represents these values is *NumLiteralCls*.

NumLiteralCls: definition.   First we specify that *NumLiteralCls* is derived from
PTreeNodeCls. Details of the C++ method for prescribing class derivation are found
in Line 33 of the following listing. The C++ reserved word *public* just indicates that
NumLiteralCls will inherit the *PTreeNodeCls* members as its own members and
retaining the same public/private specification as they had in the base class.

```
NumLiteralCls Definition (p_tree.h)

 32 typedef class NumLiteralCls   *PNumLiteralCls;
 33 class NumLiteralCls : public PTreeNodeCls {
 34     public:
 35          NumLiteralCls();
 36          int              get_value()
 37                                {return value;}
 38     private:
 39          int              value;
 40 };
```

Then we need to determine the data members needed by all objects and the class
functions that must provide the necessary behaviors. In this case there is one
constructor *NumLiteralCls()*, a member function *get_value()*, and since the only
possible values in the example compiler are of integer type, one integer data member
for storing the value.

8.5   IdentCls

IdentCls: definition.   The class definition for *IdentCls* below contains the usual
constructor *IdentCls()* and a function *get_name()* that returns the string valued
identifier lexeme associated with each *IdentCls* object.

```
IdentCls Definition (p_tree.h)

 42 typedef class IdentCls   *PIdentCls;
 43 class IdentCls : public PTreeNodeCls {
 44     public:
 45          IdentCls();
 46          char              *get_name();
 47 };
```

The class definition need not contain a private member for storing the identifier
string, since *IdentCls* is derived from *PTreeNodeCls* that itself contains a member
pointing to the corresponding *LexTokCls* object generated by the scanner.

8.6   ExprCls

Grammar productions 56–71 (page 76) indicate that expressions consist only of
factors and that factors come in two flavors: those consisting of numeric literals
(production 59–60) and those consisting of a reference to a variable (productions
59–62). In the mature version of the compiler, expressions are comprised of factors,
terms, and a special class of simple expressions.

```
ExprCls Definition (p_tree.h)

49 typedef class ExprCls  *PExprCls;
50 class ExprCls : public PTreeNodeCls {
51    public:
52          ExprCls();
53          virtual int        evaluate();
54          virtual int        emit();
55    protected:
56          int value;
57 };
```

```
FactorCls Definition (p_tree.h)

59 typedef class FactorCls *PFactorCls;
60 class FactorCls : public ExprCls {
61   public:
62          FactorCls();
63 };
65 typedef class NumFactorCls *PNumFactorCls;
66 class NumFactorCls : public FactorCls {
67   public:
68          NumFactorCls(PPTreeNodeCls NumLit);
69          int             evaluate();
70          int             emit();
71 };
73
74
75 typedef class VarAccessFactorCls *PVarAccessFactorCls;
76 class VarAccessFactorCls : public FactorCls {
77   public:
78          VarAccessFactorCls(PPTreeNodeCls Ident);
79          int             evaluate();
80          int             emit();
81   private:
82          PPTreeNodeCls ident;
83 };
```

ExprCls: definitions.   There are two things that make up expressions: the type of
an expression and the current value. Since integer is the only type in this example
compiler, *ExprCls* contains only the integer-valued member *value*. Expressions must
be evaluated during program execution. The member function *evaluate()* returns
the integer value of any parse tree node derived from *ExprCls*.

FactorCls is derived from *ExprCls*, as suggested by production 56 in the grammar. In this example compiler, *FactorCls* is the base class for *NumFactorCls* and *VarAccessFactorCls*.

VarAccessFactorCls contains the private member *ident* so that a symbol table lookup can be made to determine the value of the corresponding variable. The C++ type for *ident* is *PPTreeNodeCls*, rather than a **char****. The reason for this is a bit involved.

- Note that the action calling the constructor *VarAccessFactorCls()* in productions 59–62 is obtaining the *IdentCls* object through the value stack variable $1.

- Recall also that all items on the parser's value stack are declared to be the base class PTreeNodeCls.

So the *Ident* argument for the *VarAccessFactorCls* constructor and the corresponding private member *ident* for the class must be of the base class type as well.

8.7   StatementCls

StatementCls: definition.   The following code contains the *StatementCls* definition. Notice that this class has two constructors, the first one called a default constructor and the second that we actually intend to call when we build the parse tree. Some versions of C++ require default constructors for classes that use the virtual (late-binding) declaration for member functions.

```
StatementCls Definition (p_tree.h)

85 typedef class StatementCls *PStatementCls;
86 class StatementCls : public PTreeNodeCls, public LstSeqBldrCls {
87     public:
88           StatementCls()  {;}
89           StatementCls(char *StmtText);
90           int             emit();
91     protected:
92           char            *stmt_text;
93 };
```

The Pascal source line corresponding to the particular *StatementCls* object is stored in the member *stmt_text*. This information is emitted as a comment in the generated assembly code during code generation. *Emit()* outputs this comment for *StatementCls*. Since no such activity occurs during program interpreting, there is no corresponding *execute()* function.

```
┌──────────────────────────────────────────────────────────────────────┐
│  ┌─────────────────────────────┐                                        │
│  │ Derived Statements (p_tree.h)│                                        │
│  └─────────────────────────────┘                                        │
│                                                                          │
│    96 typedef class EmptyStmtCls *PEmptyStmtCls;                         │
│    97 class EmptyStmtCls : public StatementCls {                         │
│    98    public:                                                         │
│    99          EmptyStmtCls()  {;}                                       │
│   100          int            execute();                                 │
│   101          int            emit();                                    │
│   102 };                                                                 │
│   104 typedef class AssignmentStmtCls *PAssignmentStmtCls;               │
│   105 class AssignmentStmtCls : public StatementCls {                    │
│   106    public:                                                         │
│   107          AssignmentStmtCls() {;}                                   │
│   108          AssignmentStmtCls(PPTreeNodeCls Ident,                    │
│   109                            PPTreeNodeCls Expr,                     │
│   110                               char* StmtText);                     │
│   111          int            execute();                                 │
│   112          int            emit();                                    │
│   113    private:                                                        │
│   114          PPTreeNodeCls  ident;        //lhs                        │
│   115          PPTreeNodeCls  expr;         //rhs                        │
│   116 };                                                                 │
│   118 typedef class WriteStmtCls *PWriteStmtCls;                         │
│   119 class WriteStmtCls : public StatementCls {                         │
│   120    public:                                                         │
│   121          WriteStmtCls()  {;}                                       │
│   122          WriteStmtCls(PPTreeNodeCls Expr,                          │
│   123                          char* StmtText);                          │
│   124          int            execute();                                 │
│   125          int            emit();                                    │
│   126    private:                                                        │
│   127          PPTreeNodeCls  expr;                                      │
│   128 };                                                                 │
└──────────────────────────────────────────────────────────────────────┘
```

StatementCls, like *ExprCls*, is derived from *PTreeNodeCls* and yet also becomes a base class for a rich collection of parse tree nodes for various Pascal statements. Productions 42–52 indicate that our compiler recognizes three kinds of Pascal statements: the empty statement (occurring most often due to statement termination rather than statement separation), the assignment statement, and the write statement. Thus we will have three kinds of statement classes derived from *StatementCls*, as defined in the listing above. These classes contain the usual constructors, including the default constructors often required by late binding of the member functions. Lines 100, 111, and 124 define respective member functions *execute()* that are called by the interpreter. The corresponding member functions *emit()* (Lines 101, 112, 125) are called by the code generator.

8.8 LstSeqBldrCls

This class encapsulates the data and behaviors supporting the construction of lists and sequences of parse tree nodes.

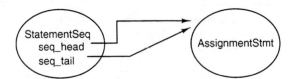

Figure 8.4. Parse Tree Sequence of One Item

LstSeqBldrCls: definition.   The definition of *LstSeqBldrCls* in the code below
consists of a constructor *LstSeqBldrCls()*, member functions *append()* and *get_next()*
and a private pointer used to store the address of the *next* item in the list.

```
LstSeqBldrCls Definition (p_tree.h)

  8 typedef class LstSeqBldrCls *PLstSeqBldrCls;
  9 class LstSeqBldrCls {
 10    public:
 11          LstSeqBldrCls();
 12          virtual PLstSeqBldrCls  append(PLstSeqBldrCls);
 13          virtual PLstSeqBldrCls  get_next()
 14                                       {return next;}
 15    private:
 16          PLstSeqBldrCls          next;
 17 };
```

LstSeqBldrCls: importance.   Of far greater importance than the class definition
and implementation information is the *manner* in which this class is used. Think
back to the preceding discussion of the construction of the parse tree, particularly
action 8.1. The members of a *StatementSeqCls* object point to a single statement as
illustrated in Figure 8.4. However, in order for the parser to add a second statement
to the list, each succeeding statement needs a corresponding pointer *next* and some
sort of function to do the appending. The object-oriented approach is to create
the needed linking functionality in another class *LstSeqBldrCls* and then to provide
this for statement objects by deriving *StatementCls* from *LstSeqBldrCls* as shown
in Figure 8.5.

8.9   StatementSeqCls

Production 36 (page 76) is responsible for creating a *StatementSeqCls* object and
placing it at the head of every sequence of *StatementCls* objects in the parse tree.
The action for production 36 requests that this *StatementSeqCls* object append the
most recently recognized statement to the existing sequence of statements. The
StatementSeqCls object certainly can point to the beginning (and the end) of the
sequence of statement nodes. But what is needed is for *StatementCls* objects to
have the ability to point to *each other* as they are being added to the list. Look

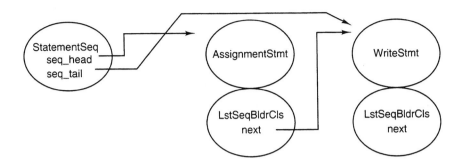

Figure 8.5. Parse Tree Sequences Using LstSeqBldrCls

closely at the definition of *StatementCls* (Section 8.7). Notice that *StatementCls* is derived from *two* base classes. This is an example of what is called **multiple inheritance**. *StatementCls* objects not only are *PTreeNodeCls* objects, but also inherit the data members behaviors of *LstSeqBldrCls*.

StatementSeqCls: definition. StatementSeqCls Definition (p_tree.h)

```
130 typedef class StatementSeqCls *PStatementSeqCls;
131 class StatementSeqCls : public PTreeNodeCls {
132    public:
133          StatementSeqCls() {;}
134          StatementSeqCls(PPTreeNodeCls Stmt);
135          int            execute();
136          int            emit();
137          PPTreeNodeCls  append(PPTreeNodeCls);
138    private:
139          StatementCls   *seq_head;
140          StatementCls   *seq_tail;
141 };
```

8.10 BlockCls

Since the example compiler deals with a very simple version of Pascal in which there are no procedures or functions, a Pascal block (production 30) occurs only in the main program (production 25). So the only purpose of *BlockCls* is to point to the sequence of statements that make up the main program.

BlockCls: definition. The definition of *BlockCls* contains the usual two constructors as well as the two public member functions *execute()* and *emit()* and the private pointer *stmt_seq* to the sequence of statements comprising the block.

BlockCls Definition (p_tree.h)

```
143 typedef class BlockCls *PBlockCls;
144 class BlockCls : public PTreeNodeCls {
145    public:
146          BlockCls()        {;}
147          BlockCls(PPTreeNodeCls StmtSeq);
148          int               execute();
149          int               emit();
150    private:
151          PPTreeNodeCls     stmt_seq;
152 };
```

8.11   ProgramCls

This is the root node of the entire parse tree, though the *PTreeCls* object described in the next section actually points to this root.

ProgramCls: definition.   The *ProgramCls* definition below contains data members (*std_table*), the program name (*ident*), and the rest of the tree (*block*).

ProgramCls Definition (p_tree.h)

```
154 typedef class ProgramCls *PProgramCls;
155 class ProgramCls : public PTreeNodeCls {
156    public:
157          ProgramCls()    {;}
158          ProgramCls(PPTreeNodeCls Ident, PPTreeNodeCls Block);
159          int               execute();
160          int               emit();
161          void              print();
162    private:
163          SymtabCls         *std_table;
164          PIdentCls         ident;
165          PPTreeNodeCls     block;
166 };
```

Std_table points to the small compiler's only symbol table. In more mature compilers, this table would be the outermost table consisting of all the Pascal standard identifiers. Other symbol tables would then be used for various identifiers found in the source code.

Ident points to the program name. In Pascal, this identifier is not as important as it is in languages supporting multiple-file compilation.

Block will be used to access the section of the parse tree representing the sequence of source statements.

8.12   PTreeCls

A *PTreeCls* object is not a parse tree node, since it is not created by any grammar production.

```
PTreeCls Definition (p_tree.h)

170 typedef class PTreeCls *PPTreeCls;
171 class PTreeCls {
172   public:
173         PTreeCls(PPTreeNodeCls Root);
174         int            execute();
175         int            emit();
176         void           print();
177   private:
178         PPTreeNodeCls  root;
179         PPTreeNodeCls  current;
180 };
```

It merely points to the *ProgramCls* object that forms the root of the parse tree.

8.13   Summary

In this chapter we have presented the definition details of the various parse tree nodes used by the example compiler.

- **PTreeNodeCls**

  This is the base class for all the parse tree classes. It contains a data member for storing the lexeme/token information recognized by any parse tree leaf object. It also contains virtual member functions that will be redefined by some or all of the derived classes.

- **NumLiteralCls**

  Numeric literals in this simple compiler are only of integer type. The integer value is therefore made a data member. A corresponding get-function returns that value.

- **IdentCls**

  IdentCls objects are also leaves on the parse tree. They do not need to maintain a special data member to store the identifier, since the parent *PTreeNodeCls* from which *IdentCls* is derived contains this information in the lexeme/token member.

- **ExprCls**

  Expressions are things that have type and value. Since expressions in the example compiler are only of integer type, *ExprCls* contains only a data member for storing the value of the expression.

Even at the simplified level of this compiler there are several different ways to build an expression. We therefore make *ExprCls* as base class by declaring the *evaluate()* and *emit()* functions as virtual.

- **NumFactorCls**

  In preparation for a more complex situation, we derived the intermediate *FactorCls* from *ExprCls* and then derived *NumFactorCls* from *FactorCls*. Numeric factors are constant expressions that can be evaluated and that need to be able to emit assembly code for locating the constant value.

- **VarAccessFactorCls**

  Identifiers used in expressions can represent many different things. This class has been defined in anticipation of that need. Its present definition, however, consists only of a data member for storing the identifier and the normal *evaluate()* and *emit()* functions that exist for all expressions.

- **StatementCls**

  StatementCls, like *ExprCls*, is a base class for the classes representing the three kinds of statements recognized by this compiler. Again, since it is a base class, its *evaluate()* and *emit()* functions are made virtual.

  - **EmptyStatmentCls**
  - **AssignmentStmtCls**
  - **WriteStmtCls**

  Since we often will need to construct a linked-list of each *StatementCls* object, the class *StatementCls* will be derived from *LstSeqBldrCls*. Then any of the three statements inherit the various members necessary for supporting the linked-list activity.

- **StatementSeqCls**

  StatementSeqCls is essentially a sentinel that sits at the head of a linked list of statements. This class therefore needs data members to point to the linked list.

- **BlockCls**

- **ProgramCls**

  This is the root of the parse tree. Its data members point to information that may be needed either by compiler objects outside of the tree.

8.14   Suggested Activities

1. Use a diagram something like Figures 8.1 and 8.2 to trace through the parse tree construction for the following program.

```
1   program Assigns;
2   begin
3       i := 1;
5       writeln(j);
4       j := i;
5       writeln(j)
6   end.
```

2. How would the example compiler behave with a program like the following?

```
1   program Assigns;
2   begin
3       i := 1;
4       j := i;
5       writeln(i,j)
6   end.
```

3. Define (but do not implement) your own version of the *p_tree* module. The following class sequence may prove helpful.

   (a) The *PTreeNodeCls* base class.

   (b) The classes representing literals used by your compiler.

   (c) *IdentCls*.

   (d) The *ExprCls* base class.

   (e) The various expression classes that your compiler uses.

   (f) The *StatementCls* base class.

   (g) The various statement classes required for your compiler.

   (h) Classes supporting the construction of linked lists in the parse tree.

   (i) The higher level classes.

Chapter 9

Implementing Parse Tree Behavior

This chapter describes the implementation of the important class constructor functions.

> When the entire right-hand side of a grammar rule has been recognized, the parse tree node representing the left-hand side will be created and stored on the parser's value stack.

In C++, a class constructor is executed whenever an object is created.

9.1 PTreeNodeCls: Header

```
Header (p_tree.C)

    5 #include <iostream.h>
    6 #include <libc.h>
    7 #include <string.h>
    8                    .
    9 #include "../scanparse/scanparse.h"
   10 #include "../symtab/symtab.h"
   11
   12 #include "p_tree.h"
   13
```

The reference to *libc.h* is required so that the ASCII-to-integer utility *atoi* can be referenced by *NumLiteralCls*. *String.h* is included so that so that *strlen* can be used.

9.2 PTreeNodeCls: The Base Class

The code in the following listing contains two ideas not yet discussed. The first is the keyword *extern*, which indicates *lex_tok* is defined elsewhere[1] in the compiler code.

---
[1] In *scanparse.C*.

95

The second idea comes from many frustrating hours of tracking down a surprisingly pervasive object-oriented bug. Suppose that we forget to define and implement an *execute()* or *emit()* function for one of the many parse tree nodes derived from *PTreeNodeCls*. Dynamic binding then plays a cruel trick on us. It very quietly invokes[2] the corresponding function for the base class, which was never intended to be called and that most certainly will not produce the intended behavior! So to warn that something is definitely amiss, the "BASE CLASS" messages are routinely placed in all virtual functions of the base class.

```
PTreeNodeCls Implementation (p_tree.C)

25 PTreeNodeCls :: PTreeNodeCls() {
26     //cout << "PTreeNodeCls" << endl;
27     extern LexTokCls *lex_tok;
28     lt = lex_tok;
29 }
30
31 int PTreeNodeCls :: emit() {
32     cout << "PTreeNodeCls::emit()  BASECLASS !!!!!!!" << endl;
33     return 0;
34 }
35
36 int PTreeNodeCls :: execute() {
37     cout << "PTreeNodeCls::execute()  BASECLASS !!!!!!!" << endl;
38     return 0;
39 }
40
41 void PTreeNodeCls :: print() {
42     //cout << "PTreeNodeCls::print() " << " lex_tok " << *lt ;
43 }
44
```

9.3   NumLiteralCls

```
NumLiteralCls Implementation (p_tree.C)

46 NumLiteralCls :: NumLiteralCls() {
47     //cout << "NumLiteralCls" << endl;
48     value = atoi(this -> PTreeNodeCls::lt -> get_lexeme());
49 }
```

Line 48 may require a few words of explanation. When a literal is recognized by the following production

```
69    Number:
70       NUMLITERALTK
```

---

[2]Later versions of C++ often have a guard against this problem. Declaring such base class functions as *pure virtual* protects against their accidental invocation.

```
71                {$$ = new NumLiteralCls();}
72        ;
```

the instruction

$$\$\$ \ = \ new \ NumLiteralCls;$$

creates a *NumLiteralCls* object and places its address on the parser's value stack. Of course, *this* is a pointer to the currently created object. So

$$this \rightarrow PTreeNodeCls :: lt$$

must be a member of *NumLiteralCls*. Certainly there is no *lt* member explicitly specified in the *NumLiteralCls* definition in Chapter 8. However, note that *NumLiteralCls* is derived from *PTreeNodeCls* and so by virtue of that derivation, any *NumLiteralCls* object implicitly has the lexeme/token member that is referenced *PTreeNodeCls::lt*.

Line 48 therefore converts the character string of digits in the *LexTokCls* object *lt* to an integer value by use of the library function *atoi* defined in the standard library *libc.h*. This value is then stored in the *NumLiteralCls* data member *value*.

9.4   IdentCls

This class gives us a good example of the way that object-oriented design interacts with class implementation. The definition of the class in Chapter 8 specified the class data members, the functions, and their arguments. However, we still need to determine the specific tasks that make up each of the behaviors.

Our first such design activity is to decide what the *IdentCls* constructor should do. A good way to do this is to carefully note how *IdentCls* is *used* by the various compiler objects. Recall that constructors are called when class objects are instantiated. In our compiler, this occurs exclusively when parser actions like

$$\$\$ = newIdentCls();$$

are executed. To see how these objects are then used, we need only to look for productions having *Identifier* in their right-hand side. There are three such grammar productions (page 76). The assignment statement (production 48) is the most important of the three, since it performs a FORTRAN-like variable declaration of identifiers in the compiler: If the identifier being recognized has not yet been encountered in the source program, then declare it as a valid integer variable. This is done by checking a symbol table for the existence of the identifier and entering it into the table if it is not found.

The use of an identifier in an expression (productions 56–64) is the next most important occurrence of *Identifier*. If the identifier has not yet been encountered here, it is because the variable has not yet occurred on the left side of any previous statement, a case of the *used but not set* error. In this part of the grammar, the

IdentCls() constructor could still use the same steps as described above, except that
the value of the variable should also be initialized to zero.[3]

The last production to use the nonterminal *Identifier* is production 25. Since the
example compiler need not check for improper use of reserved words and identifiers,
the previously stated activities for the *IdentCls* constructor also remain valid here.

In light of this discussion, it is clear that the constructor *IdentCls()* should
therefore do the following:

- Get the identifier lexeme from the *LexTokCls* object associated with the
  recognized token IDENTIFIERTK.

- If the identifier has not already been declared:

  - Create a symbol table entry for the identifier.

  - Initialize the corresponding value member to zero.

  - Insert the symbol table entry into the symbol table.

These activities lead us to the second important fact about *IdentCls*: it is a good
example of component-dependency in a system and gives us a picture of the way
such dependency frequently enters into our designs. How will *IdentCls* objects know
if an identifier has already been declared, and how will the initial declarations take
place? *IdentCls()* must be able to communicate with symbol table objects. And
how will symbol table objects know what kind of entries to store? They will have to
use the *IdentCls* objects and other grammar-generated information. Both of these
classes need to be developed in the compiler at the same time!

```
IdentCls Implementation (p_tree.C)

 51 IdentCls :: IdentCls() {
 52     //cout << "IdentCls" << endl;
 53     char *name = this -> PTreeNodeCls::lt -> get_lexeme();
 54
 55     PSymtabCls scp = ScopeCls::get_vista();
 56     PSymtabEntryCls found_it = scp -> lookup(name);
 57     if (!found_it) {
 58         PVarAttCls va = new VarAttCls(name,0);
 59         scp -> insert(va);
 60     }
 61 }
 62
 63 char *IdentCls :: get_name() {
 64     //cout << "IdentCls::get_name()" << endl;
 65     return this -> PTreeNodeCls::lt -> get_lexeme();
 66 }
```

---

[3] The additional initialization would cause no trouble for the action needed in production 48.

The member references in line 53 are just like those for *NumLiteralCls* described earlier. The expression

$$this \;\rightarrow\; PTreeNodeCls :: lt$$

is the address of the *LexTokCls* object containing the identifier lexeme. So

$$this \;\rightarrow\; PTreeNodeCls :: lt \;\rightarrow\; get\_lexeme()$$

is the actual identifier string. In line 55 *scp* gets the address of the compiler's only symbol table, and thus the expression *scp* $\rightarrow$ *lookup(name)* requests that the table **scp* look up *name* and return a pointer to the table entry if the name already exists in the table. If the entry does *not* exist (line 57), the identifier is entered into the table by first creating a variable attribute symbol table entry *va* and then requesting **scp* to do the insertion.

The *IdentCls* member function *get_name()* returns the string information of the identifier stored in the *LexTokCls* object **lt*.

9.5   ExprCls

The following C++ code contains the standard fare for base classes: simple constructors and not-to-be-executed virtual functions.

```
ExprCls Implementation (p_tree.C)

68 ExprCls :: ExprCls() {
69     //cout << "ExprCls" << endl;
70 }
71
72 int ExprCls :: evaluate() {
73     cout << "ExprCls::evaluate()  BASE CLASS !!!!!!!" << endl;
74     return 0;
75 }
76
77 int ExprCls :: emit() {
78     cout << "ExprCls::emit()  BASE CLASS !!!!!!!" << endl;
79     return 0;
80 }
81
82 FactorCls :: FactorCls() {
83     //cout << "FactorCls() " << endl;
84 }
```

The implementation details for *NumFactorCls* below are also quite standard for derived classes.

NumFactor Implementation (p_tree.C)

```
86 NumFactorCls :: NumFactorCls(PPTreeNodeCls NumLit) {
87      //cout << "NumFactorCls() " << endl;
88      if (!NumLit) {
89          cerr << "NumFactorCls - LOGIC ERROR" << endl;
90      }
91      ExprCls::value = PNumLiteralCls(NumLit) -> get_value();
92      //cout << " value " << ExprCls::value << endl;
93 }
94
95 int NumFactorCls :: evaluate() {
96      //cout << "NumFactorCls::evaluate()" << endl;
97      return ExprCls::value;
98 }
99
100 VarAccessFactorCls :: VarAccessFactorCls(PPTreeNodeCls Ident) {
101      //cout << "VarAccessFactorCls() " << endl;
```

Lines 88 and 89 contain antibugging code that is often helpful in assuring correctness of grammar actions. Grammar calls to constructors that result in NULL values for pointers cause segmentation or bus errors when lines like 91 are executed. Line 91 also involves recasting the *PTreeNodeCls* pointer *NumLit* to a *NumLiteralCls* pointer.

VarAccessFactorCls Implementation (p_tree.C)

```
100 VarAccessFactorCls :: VarAccessFactorCls(PPTreeNodeCls Ident) {
101      //cout << "VarAccessFactorCls() " << endl;
102      if (!Ident) {
103          cerr << "VarAccessFactorCls() - LOGIC ERROR" << endl;
104      }
105      ident = Ident;
106      char *name = PIdentCls(ident) -> get_name();
107      PSymtabCls scp = ScopeCls::get_vista();
108      PSymtabEntryCls found_it = scp -> lookup(name);
109      if (!found_it) {
110          cerr << "        " << *name << " used but not set" << endl;
111          PVarAttCls va = new VarAttCls(name,0);
112          scp -> insert(va);
113          ExprCls::value = 0;
114      } else {
115          ExprCls::value = PVarAttCls(found_it) -> get_value();
116      }
117 }
118
119 int VarAccessFactorCls :: evaluate() {
120      //cout << "VarAccessFactorCls::evaluate()" << endl;
121      char *name = PIdentCls(ident) -> get_name();
122      PSymtabCls scp = ScopeCls::get_vista();
123      PSymtabEntryCls found_it = scp -> lookup(name);
124      return  PVarAttCls(found_it) -> get_value();
125 }
```

The constructor for *VarAccessFactorCls* contains code for initializing its data member *ident* (line 105) and for initializing the member *value* from the base class *ExprCls* (lines 113 and 115). The member function *VarAccessCls :: evaluate()* returns the value stored in the corresponding identifier's symbol table entry, *scp → lookup(name)*. These *evaluate()* functions are called during the interpreting of the source program.

9.6   StatementCls

Implementation details for the statement class constructors are listed below.

```
StatementCls Implementation (p_tree.C)

128 StatementCls :: StatementCls(char *StmtText) {
129     //cout << "StatementCls()" << endl;
130     stmt_text = new char[strlen(StmtText)+1];
131     strcpy(stmt_text,StmtText);
132 }
133
134 AssignmentStmtCls :: AssignmentStmtCls(
135                         PPTreeNodeCls Ident,
136                         PPTreeNodeCls Expr,
137                           char* TextLine):
138                               StatementCls(TextLine) {
139     //cout << "AssignmentStmtCls() " << endl;
140     if (!Ident || !Expr) {
141         cerr << "AssignmentStmtCls() - LOGIC ERROR " << endl;
142     }
143     ident = Ident;
144     expr = Expr;
145 }
146
147 WriteStmtCls :: WriteStmtCls(PPTreeNodeCls Expr,
148                           char* TextLine):
149                               StatementCls(TextLine) {
150     //cout << "WriteStmtCls() " << endl;
151     if (!Expr) {
152         cerr << "WriteStmtCls() - LOGIC ERROR " << endl;
153     }
154     expr = Expr;
155 }
```

The third line of the *StatementCls* constructor sets aside space for the original source text. The next line stores the text in *stmt_text*.

There is an important constructor detail in the header lines for *AssignmentStmtCls()* and *WriteStmtCls()*. When a C++ object of a derived class is created, a constructor for the base class is first automatically called, followed by a constructor for the derived class. Since the base class may have many constructors, the mechanism for selecting the particular base constructor is the colon (lines 137 and 148) followed by the invocation of the base constructor selected by a particular argument value.

9.7   LstSeqBldrCls

The code for the simple constructor, *LstSeqBldrCls()* and the member function
append() are listed below.

```
┌─────────────────────────────────────────────────────┐
│ LstSeqBldrCls Implementation (p_tree.C)              │
│                                                       │
│   14 LstSeqBldrCls :: LstSeqBldrCls() {               │
│   15      //cout << "LstSeqBldrCls()" << endl;        │
│   16      next = 0;                                    │
│   17 }                                                 │
│   18                                                   │
│   19 PLstSeqBldrCls LstSeqBldrCls ::                  │
│   20                      append(PLstSeqBldrCls ToBeAdded) { │
│   21      //cout << "LstSeqBldrCls::append()" << endl; │
│   22      return this -> next = ToBeAdded;            │
│   23 }                                                 │
└─────────────────────────────────────────────────────┘
```

The variable *this* just contains the address of the particular *LstSeqBldrCls* object;
so the code

$$this \rightarrow next = ToBeAdded$$

just assigns the address presently in *ToBeAdded* to the object's data member *next*.

9.8   StatementSeqCls

```
┌─────────────────────────────────────────────────────────────┐
│ StatementSeqCls Implementation (p_tree.C)                    │
│                                                               │
│  158 StatementSeqCls :: StatementSeqCls (PPTreeNodeCls Stmt) { │
│  159      //cout << "StatementSeqCls() " << endl;             │
│  160      seq_tail = seq_head = PStatementCls(Stmt);          │
│  161 }                                                         │
│  162                                                           │
│  163 PPTreeNodeCls StatementSeqCls :: append(PPTreeNodeCls Stmt) { │
│  164      //cout << "StatementSeqCls::append()" << endl;      │
│  165      if (!seq_tail) {                                     │
│  166         cerr << "StatementSeqCls::append() -- LOGIC ERROR" << endl; │
│  167      } else {                                             │
│  168         seq_tail = PStatementCls(seq_tail ->             │
│  169                      LstSeqBldrCls::append(PStatementCls(Stmt))); │
│  170      }                                                    │
│  171      return this;                                         │
│  172 }                                                         │
└─────────────────────────────────────────────────────────────┘
```

The *StatementSeqCls* constructor receives as its argument a pointer to the first
statement in the sequence, so it makes sense to have *seq_head* and *seq_tail* both
point to this statement tree node. The *append()* member function changes the
StatementSeqCls object's member *seq_tail* to point to the appended statement (lines
168 and 169).[4]

---

[4] This works because *StatementCls::append()* will return the address of the statement just added
to the list.

9.9   BlockCls

```
┌─────────────────────────────────────────┐
│ BlockCls Implementation (p_tree.C) │
└─────────────────────────────────────────┘

175 BlockCls :: BlockCls(PPTreeNodeCls StmtSeq) {
176     //cout << "BlockCls" << endl;
177     stmt_seq = StmtSeq;
178 }
```

Similar trivial code will not be included in the later portions of the text. You will
easily be able to produce such code or can locate it in Appendix A.

9.10   ProgramCls

There is a rather significant idea contained in the following implementation code.

```
┌─────────────────────────────────────────┐
│ ProgramCls Implementation (p_tree.C │
└─────────────────────────────────────────┘

181 extern PPTreeNodeCls prgm_node; //declared in scanparse.C
182 ProgramCls :: ProgramCls(PPTreeNodeCls Ident, PPTreeNodeCls Block) {
183     //cout << "ProgramCls() " << endl;
184     ident = PIdentCls(Ident);
185     block = PBlockCls(Block);
186     std_table = ScopeCls::get_vista();
187     prgm_node = this;
188 }
189
190 void ProgramCls::print() {
191     cout << "ProgramCls::print()" << endl;
192 }
```

Since we are using a parser (Chapter 6) that builds the tree from the leaves up
toward the root, trying to move down the tree or to point to the actual tree root
becomes a bit of a task. The usual way to solve this problem in C and C++ is
through the use of global variables. Because the parser actually builds the tree, the
ScanParseCls object must keep track of the parse tree root (and thus the entire
tree). The first line actually declares *prgm_node* to be a systemwide global variable,
since it is outside any function in the *scanparse.C*. Line 187 then makes that global
variable point to the root of the tree, dangerous code indeed.

   This same kind of problem is solved in a more tasteful manner in Line 186,
where global-encapsulating *ScopeCls* is used to make *std_table* point to the symbol
table object that was created in another module and therefore not readily accessible
in this one.

9.11   PTreeCls

```
PTreeCls Implementation (p_tree.C)

197 PTreeCls :: PTreeCls(PPTreeNodeCls Root) {
198     //cout << "PTreeCls()" << endl;
199     root = current = Root;
200 }
201
202 void PTreeCls :: print() {
203     cout << "PTreeCls " << endl;
204     root -> print();
205 }
```

9.12   Module Makefile

Actually, the following makefile only builds a part of the *p_tree* module.

```
p_tree/Makefile

 1 #Makefile for Pascal compiler parse tree nodes
 2 PROGRAM: p_tree.o
 3
 4 p_tree.o:       ../scanparse/scanparse.h ../symtab/symtab.h\
 5                 p_tree.h p_tree.C
 6                 CC -c -g p_tree.C
 7
 8 clean:
 9                 rm -f *.o a.out
10
11 print:
12                 /usr/5bin/pr -n p_tree.h p_tree.C Makefile > p_tree.lst
13                 a2ps p_tree.lst | lpr -Pmlw
14                 rm -f p_tree.lst
15
16 count:
17                 wc *.h *.C Makefile
```

There are *execute()* member functions of the various parse tree classes that are implemented in the *interp* submodule (Chapter 10). Similarly, the *emit()* member functions of the tree nodes are implemented in the *emitter* submodule (Chapter 11). Each of these submodules has its own makefile.

9.13   Suggested Activities

1. Test your *p_tree* module by writing sample Pascal programs that will exercise each production in your grammar. You can test at least the order of creation of parse tree objects by turning on the output messages at the beginning of each constructor.

2. *LstSeqBldrCls* is used not only for representing sequences of statements in a parse tree but also for a number of other very important list structures. One such application is the construction of the list of identifiers that may be used in a Pascal variable declaration.

   (a) Modify your grammar to be able to recognize a list of identifiers that are separated by commas.

   (b) Define and implement an *IdentLstCls* parse tree class.

   (c) Modify the definition of *IdentCls* to allow for a **list** of *ExprCls* objects. *Suggestion*: this is where *LstSeqBldrCls* is used.

   (d) Test your program.

3. In Activity 8 of Chapter 6 you extended the grammar to include some selection statement. Define and implement the corresponding parse tree classes.

4. *NumLiteralCls* allows only for integer-valued numerical literals.

   (a) Define two subclasses, *IntLiteralCls* and *RealLiteralCls*, that could be used to represent the two different types of numerical literals in the parse tree.

   (b) Implement *IntLiteralCls* and *RealLiteralCls*, being careful to impose some elementary semantic restriction on the values of each of the two types of literals.

   (c) Incorporate these new classes into an extended compiler. Test your compiler on several source programs. Make special note of the kind of error messages that you might want to report in regard to this part of the compiler.

5. Explain why the constructor *IdentCls()* is able to access *PTreeNodeCls::lt*. You may want to consult a C++ text like Lippman [8].

6. As you read the implementation code for *ExprCls*, a nagging question begins to surface: Why all those recasting operators? In line 86 of the implementation code for *NumFactorCls*, the argument *NumLit* is typed as a pointer to *PPTreeNodeCls* and later (line 91) recast to a pointer to a NumLiteralCls. Why not just declare the argument to be of type *PNumLiteralCls* in the first place?

   Suggestion: The answer is related to parser issues. How is the parser's value stack typed?

7. List the way or ways in which the grammar influences the definition of the various classes of parse tree nodes. What kinds of changes to the grammar would induce changes to parse tree nodes?

8. Extend the compiler by adding one of the following capabilities.

(a) Declaration of (integer) variables.

Suggestion: Modify the grammar to allow the **var** section, create a declaration class that enters variables into the symbol table, and modify existing *PTreeNodeCls* constructors so that they do not enter a variable in the usual FORTRAN fashion.

(b) Extend expressions to include the usual add operations and multiply operations.

Suggestion: Modify grammar to allow for new operations. Create operation classes that can be used to represent the operations in the parse tree. Implement *evaluate()* functions for these classes.

(c) Add the type **real**. This will allow you to experiment a bit with your scanner specification.

Suggestion: You can add this feature even if your compiler does not recognize the **var** declaration structures. Do you see how?

(d) Add one of the following Pascal statements.

 i. An **if/else** statement. Note this will introduce a shift/reduce conflict to the grammar. Don't worry about the message.

 ii. A **while** statement.

 iii. A **for** statement.

Chapter 10

Interpreter Module

When interpreting a source program, statements *execute()*.

10.1 Statements

Execute() for Statement Classes (interp.C)

```
10 int EmptyStmtCls :: execute() {
11     //cout << "EmptyStmtCls::execute()" << endl;
12     return 0;
13 }
14
15 int AssignmentStmtCls :: execute() {
16     //cout << "AssignmentStmtCls::execute() " << endl;
17     int rval = PExprCls(expr) -> evaluate();
18
19     char *name = PIdentCls(ident) -> get_name();
20     PSymtabCls scp = ScopeCls::get_vista();
21     PSymtabEntryCls found_it = scp -> lookup(name);
22     if (!found_it) {
23         cout << "AssignmentStmtCls::execute() LOGIC ERROR" << endl;
24         //should be done with an ErrorCls object
25     } else {
26         PVarAttCls(found_it) -> set_value(rval);
27     }
28     return 0;
29 }
30
31 int WriteStmtCls :: execute() {
32     //cout << "WriteStmtCls::execute() " << expr << endl;
33     cout << "   -> " << PExprCls(expr) -> evaluate() << endl;
34     return 0;
35 }
```

These functions return a value indicating the success of their activity:

- 0: Indicates that the statement executed normally.

- 1: Indicates that a semantic error or terminating condition[1] has been encountered during execution.

EmptyStmtCls::execute() does not have much to do, obviously. *AssignmentStmt-Cls::execute()* must calculate the value *rval* of the right-hand side *expr* of the statement[2] and then store this value in the symbol table entry associated with the variable member *ident* on the left-hand side of the assignment. *WriteStmt-Cls::execute()* just outputs the evaluated value of the expression in line 33.

10.2   Statement Sequences

```
 StatementSeqCls :: execute() (interp.C)

 37 int StatementSeqCls :: execute() {
 38     //cout << "StatementSeqCls::execute() " << endl;
 39     PPTreeNodeCls p = this -> seq_head;
 40     while (p) {
 41         p -> execute();
 42         p = PStatementCls(PStatementCls(p) -> get_next());
 43     }
 44     return 0;
 45 }
```

The short segment of code for *StatementSeqCls* above contains a nice example of late binding and of the use of inherited members. Remember that

$$this \; \rightarrow \; seq\_head$$

points to the first *StatementCls* object in the list of statements. So, *p*, whoever you are, execute yourself (line 41) and then replace yourself with your neighbor (line 42). More mature compiler versions would examine the value returned by

$$p \; \rightarrow \; execute()$$

in line 41 for execution codes that might signal breaking out of the (C++ while) loop.

---

[1] Some languages allow programmers to exit from loops or subprograms, quite apart from program termination due to error conditions. In these languages, a returned value of 1 is usually used for the normal terminating signal, while higher integer values indicate the various error conditions requiring program termination.

[2] In normal object-oriented fashion, the expression is evaluated by late binding. Whatever kind of *ExprCls* object you are in line 17, *evaluate()* yourself!

10.3   Higher Level Classes

```
execute() for Higher Classes (interp.C)

47 int BlockCls :: execute() {
48     //cout << "BlockCls::execute() " << endl;
49     return this -> stmt_seq -> execute();
50 }
51
52 int ProgramCls :: execute() {
53     //cout << "ProgramCls::execute() " << endl;
54     return this -> block -> execute();
55 }
56
57 int PTreeCls :: execute() {
58     //cout << "PTreeCls::execute() " << endl;
59     if (!root) {
60         cerr << "PTreeCls::execute - LOGIC ERROR" << endl;
61         return 0;
62     } else {
63         return root -> execute();
64     }
```

Lines 59–61 are just another form of the C++ antibugging code described earlier,
which always tests a pointer before dereferencing it. Compiler performance could
probably be improved by deleting these tests, but only after the parser logic has
been well exercised and has gained a reputation for being reasonably free from such
errors.

10.4   Makefile

```
interp/Makefile

 1 #Makefile for Pascal interpretor
 2 PROGRAM: interp.o
 3
 4 interp.o:       ../symtab/symtab.h ../p_tree/p_tree.h interp.C
 5         CC -c -g interp.C
 6
 7 clean:
 8         rm -f *.o tmp* a.out
 9
10 print:
11         /usr/5bin/pr -n interp.C Makefile > Interp.lst
12         a2ps Interp.lst | lpr -Pmlw
13         rm -f Interp.lst
14
15 count:
16         wc *.C Makefile
```

10.5   Suggested Activities

1. In this chapter we have discussed the implementation of *execute()* for the following classes.

   - EmptyStmtCls
   - AssignmentStmtCls
   - WriteStmtClS
   - StatementSeqCls
   - BlockCls
   - ProgramCls
   - PTreeCls

   For each one, describe or summarize in words the implementation details.

2. Implement your own versions of the various *execute()* member functions.

3. Test your compiler on the following kinds of statements.

   (a) A program consisting only of the empty statement.

   (b) A **writeln** statement outputting the value of a literal.

   (c) An assignment statement. Test this by also including a writeln statement outputting the value of the variable used in the assignment statement.

4. In Activity 8 of Chapter 6 you extended your grammar to include some selection statement such as the Pascal *if* statement. In Activity 3 of Chapter 9 you defined and implemented the corresponding parse tree classes.

   (a) Complete the implementation of those classes by coding the *execute()* and *evaluate()* functions that are necessary to supporting interpreting this new statement.

   (b) Carefully test your extended compiler. Be sure to test it on programs that are boundary (albeit still valid) examples.

5. Construct a more traditional interpreter: Write and test a function that traverses the parse tree, executing as it goes. Compare this approach with the object-oriented method described in the text.

   (a) Code size

   (b) Code complexity

   (c) Coding time

   (d) Execution time

Chapter 11

Emitter Module

11.1 Chapter Overview

This last chapter contains the implementation details of the function *emit()* for those parse tree nodes involved in code generation.

Recall that our compiler must output a file containing valid SPARCstation assembly language code, which is then converted to an executable file, *a.out*. Each of the major objects of the parse tree needs to emit assembler code that corresponds to the behavior(s) associated with that node.

- In the case of those objects related to the declaration of variables, the code emitted is just an assembly language declaration of data. This is described in Section 11.3.

- Parse tree nodes representing an expression must emit assembly code that evaluates that expression. The corresponding expression value must be placed in a program location that will be accessible to the higher level expressions or statements accessing that value. Section 11.4 contains the implementation details for these ideas.

- Parse tree nodes representing the various program statements must emit assembly language instructions that perform those instructions. These ideas are described in Section 11.6.

11.2 A Simple Example

Before looking at the particular assembly language code associated with each parse tree node, we want to trace through the code production for the following example.

```
Example Program

1    program simple;
2    begin
3        j := 3;
4        i := j;
5        writeln(i)
6    end.
```

111

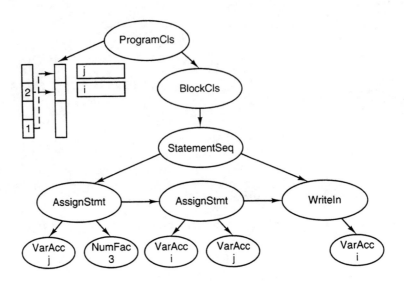

Figure 11.1. Parse Tree for Example Program

The compiler first translates this program into a parse tree. The tree is then translated into an assembly language program that is then assembled and linked with any supporting system functions into an executable.

11.2.1   Parse tree

The parse tree that the compiler creates to represent the example program would look essentially like the one illustrated in Figure 11.1.

11.2.2   Corresponding Assembly Language Program

Most assembly language programs are structured into various control sections or **segments**. SPARC ® assembly language (see Paul [9]) allows for a text segment, an initialized data section and an uninitialized data section,as illustrated in Figure 11.2.

- **Text segment.** The **Text segment.** is the address space in the assembled program that will contain executable machine instructions. The *.text* statements in the assembly language program specify the segment into which the final assembled instructions should be loaded.

- **Data segment.** The **data segment** is the address space where initialized data is placed.

- **bss segment.** The **bss segment** is the address space where the uninitialized data areas are placed.

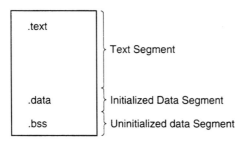

Figure 11.2. Assembly Language Program Format

A particular SPARC Ⓡ assembly program corresponding to the source program could then have the following form.

```
 Corresponding assembly language program

    1              .text
    2              .global _main
    3
    4    _main:
    5              save    %sp,-MINWINDOW,%sp
    6    !    j := 3
    7              mov     0x3,%o0
    8              sethi   %hi(_j),%o1
    9              st      %o0,[%o1+%lo(_j)]
   10    !    i := j
   11              sethi   %hi(_j),%o0
   12              ld      [%o0+%lo(_j)],%o0
   13              sethi   %hi(_i),%o1
   14              st      %o0,[%o1+%lo(_i)]
   15    !    writeln(i)
   16              sethi   %hi(_i),%o0
   17              ld      [%o0+%lo(_i)],%o0
   18              call    _Writeln,1
   19              nop
   20              ret
   21              restore %o0, 0, %o0
   22
   23              .data
   24    #define DW(x)    (((x)+7)&(~0x07))
   25    #define MINFRAME ((16+1+6)*4)
   26              MINWINDOW = 96 /* DW(MINFRAME) */
   27
   28              .bss
   29              .align  4
   30              .common _j,4
   31              .align  4
   32              .common _i,4
```

The *.global* directive indicates that _*main* is a symbol that is accessible outside the program in which it is defined. This access is by the linker, which needs to be able to see this symbol, since it is the one usually executed.

The *save* instruction is used to create a new stack frame for the program. On SPARCs, the minimal stack frame size in words is 92. This must be rounded up to the next double word boundary of 96, as noted in the data segment.

Each of the three statements are then emulated by corresponding assembly language instructions. Details on these instructions are found in Section 11.5.

Finally, space is reserved for the various program variables in the *bss* segment.

11.2.3   Generating the Program

Now let's describe the process by which the assembly program is produced. Instead of having a single code generator that produces the code as it traverses the parse tree, we have chosen to provide each of the parse tree nodes with an *emit()* function and then to ask the tree to emit itself, just as we did for program interpreting.

The assembly language code production therefore begins when the *ControllerCls* object sends the *emit()* message to the parse tree. The parse tree object passes this message directly to the *ProgramCls* root node, which then begins the following activities.

1. The program node first outputs assembler code, which declares the code to be a program called _*main*.

2. The program node then asks the block node to emit its code. Each statement in the block is then asked to emit its own code. Assignment statements request that their expressions emit code for finding their value (if they are on the right side) or storing their value (if they are on the left). A writeln statement requests its expression to emit code for finding its value and then issues a call to a system program for outputting that value.

3. The program node outputs the wrap-up code for normal termination of _*main*, restoring the original stack frame.

4. Finally, the program node directs the symbol table to emit assembler code for the declaration of each variable in the symbol table.

11.3   Emitting Symbol Table Entries

In the case of this small compiler, all variables are of integer type. The following assembly code can be used to declare an integer variable

$$.align \qquad 4 \qquad\qquad\qquad (11.1)$$

$$.common \quad \_ < ident >, 4 \qquad\qquad (11.2)$$

where _ < *ident* > is an underscore-preceded variable name. The underscore is a device used by most C compilers for the internal representation of identifiers. Using the same convention for this compiler allows the code generated by the compiler to be linked with programs written in C.

```
Symbol Table Code Generator (emit.C)

 9 int VarAttCls :: emit() {
10      //cout << "VarAttCls::emit()" << endl;
11      cout << "   .align  4" << endl;
12      cout << "   .common _" << SymtabEntryCls::name;
13      cout << ",4" << endl;
14      return 0;
15 }
16
17 int SymtabCls :: emit() {
18      //cout << "SymtabCls::emit()" << endl;
19
20      cout << "   .bss" << endl;
21      //First (i=1) SymtabEntryCls object is for program name
22      for (int i=2; i < next_location; i++) {
23          symtab[i] -> emit();
24      }
25      return 0;
26 }
```

Lines 11 and 12 output the assembly instructions in 11.2 for a given *SymtabEntryCls* object. At this stage of development the assembly code is sent to the normal *stdout* channel. This output can be redirected to a file for verification and additional testing.

Emitting the entire symbol table is achieved by the loop in lines 22–24 which just requests each symbol table entry (except the first one that represents the program name) to go through the emitting process described directly above.

11.4 Expressions

As previously noted, parse tree nodes representing an expression must emit assembly code that evaluates the expression and places the corresponding integer value in a predictable assembly program location. The standard location for storing such a value is the first of a special set of value registers

$$\%o0, \%o1, \%o2, \ldots$$

called *output registers*.

There are only two expressions for the example compiler: One kind of expression node represents an integer literal; the other expression represents the value of an integer variable. Evaluating the first kind of node clearly just amounts to producing assembly code that moves an integer literal to a particular register. In the following code

$$mov \quad 0x < val >, \%o0$$

the literal value is *moved* to the %o0 register. The notation $0x < val >$ just represents the hexadecimal equivalent of the integer value. *NumLiteralCls* emits this assembly code in lines 32 and 33 of the following code.

```
Code Generator for Expressions (emit.C)

30 int NumFactorCls :: emit() {
31     //cout << "NumFactorCls::emit()" << endl;
32     cout << "    mov     0x" << hex <<
33                     ExprCls::value << ",%o0" << endl;
34     return 0;
35 }
36 int VarAccessFactorCls :: emit() {
37     //cout << "VarAccessFactorCls::emit()" << endl;
38     char *ident_str = PIdentCls(ident) -> get_name();
39     cout << "    sethi   %hi(_" ;
40         cout << ident_str;
41         cout << "),%o0" << endl;
42     cout << "    ld      [%o0+%lo(_" ;
43         cout << ident_str;
44         cout << ")],%o0" << endl;
45     return 0;
46 }
```

The second kind of (variable) expression is evaluated by moving the contents of the variable's memory location to the appropriate register. The assembly code for moving the integer value of a variable to register %o0 is given by

$$sethi \qquad \%hi(\_ < ident >), \%o0 \qquad\qquad (11.3)$$

$$ld \quad [\%o0 + \%lo(\_ < ident >)], \%o0 \qquad\qquad (11.4)$$

where $\_ < ident >$ is the internal form of the variable. Lines 39–45 output the commands in 11.4 for *VarAccessFactorCls*.

11.5   StatementCls

The assembly code for calling an external routine to output the value stored in register %o0 is given by the following.

$$call \quad \_Writeln, 1 \qquad\qquad (11.5)$$

$$nop \qquad\qquad (11.6)$$

Lines 77–78 in the following C++ code output these assembly commands. Writeln() is a simple C function that is described in Section 11.7, below.

```
     ┌─────────────────────────────────────────────────────┐
     │ Emit() for Statement Classes (emit.C) │
     └─────────────────────────────────────────────────────┘
     48 int StatementCls :: emit() {
     49     cout << "! " << stmt_text << endl;
     50     return 0;
     51 }
     52
     53 int EmptyStmtCls :: emit() {
     54     //cout << "EmptyStmtCls::emit()" << endl;
     55     return 0;
     56 }
     57
     58 int AssignmentStmtCls :: emit() {
     59     //cout << "AssignmentStmtCls::emit()" << endl;
     60     StatementCls::emit();
     61     expr -> emit();
     62
     63     char *ident_str = PIdentCls(ident) -> get_name();
     64     cout << "    sethi   %hi(_" ;
     65        cout << ident_str;
     66        cout << "),%o1" << endl;
     67     cout << "    st      %o0,[%o1+%lo(_";
     68        cout << ident_str;
     69        cout << ")]" << endl;
     70     return 0;
     71 }
     72
     73 int WriteStmtCls :: emit() {
     74     //cout << "WriteStmtCls::emit()" << endl;
     75     StatementCls::emit();
     76     expr -> emit();
     77     cout << "    call  _Writeln,1" << endl;
     78     cout << "    nop" << endl;
     79     return 0;
     80 }
```

An assignment statement takes the value in the right-hand expression and stores it in the variable on the left-hand side of the assignment operator. Assembly code for moving the contents of register $\%o0$[1] to the location referenced by an identifier is as follows.

$$sethi \qquad \%hi(\_<ident>), \%o1 \qquad\qquad (11.7)$$

$$st \quad \%o0, [\%o1 + \%lo(\_<ident>)] \qquad\qquad (11.8)$$

Line 61 emits code to evaluate the expression on the right side of the assignment statement. Lines 64–69 then output the assembly code for the assignment.

Both *WriteStmtCls::emit()* and *AssignmentStmtCls::emit()* call the base class function *StatementCls::emit()* (lines 75 and 60) to output a comment line into the assembly code describing the actual statement.

---

[1]Remember that each expression emits assembly code that leaves its value in $\%o0$.

The code for *StatementSeqCls::emit()* then uses the standard loop, marching down the statements in the sequence and requesting each of them to do their special *emit()*.

```
StatementSeqCls :: emit() (emit.C)

82 int StatementSeqCls :: emit() {
83     //cout << "StatementSeqCls::emit() " << endl;
84     PPTreeNodeCls p = this -> seq_head;
85     while (p) {
86         p -> emit();
87         p = PStatementCls(PStatementCls(p) -> get_next());
88     }
89     return 0;
90 }
```

11.6   Higher Level Classes

Think about what a parse tree looks like: The *PTreeCls* object is at the very top; the *ProgramCls* tree root node comes next; the *BlockCls* is next; and then the various statement and expression nodes.

Recall that *PTreeCls::root* points to the *ProgramCls* root object for the parse tree. The *emit()* for *PTreeCls* just requests the tree root object to *emit()* (line 132).

```
emit() PTreeCls (emit.C)

121 int PTreeCls :: emit() {
122     //cout << "PTreeCls::emit() " << endl;
123     if (! root) {
124         cerr << "PTreeCls::emit - LOGIC ERROR" << endl;
125         return 0;
126     } else {
127         return root -> emit();
128     }
129 }
```

The next segment of C++ implementation code is for *ProgramCls::emit()*. Its first task is to output assembly code common to the beginning of all emitted programs (lines 100–104). Recall that *save* just initializes a stack frame for use by the program. Then *BlockCls* object is requested to *emit()* its code (i.e., the statements in that block). Finally, assembly code is produced in lines 106–114 for the normal termination of the emitted program.

```
    emit() ProgramCls (emit.C)

 97 int ProgramCls :: emit() {
 98     //cout << "ProgramCls::emit() " << endl;
 99     if (block && std_table) {
100         cout << "        .text" << endl;
101         cout << "        .global _main" << endl << endl;
102
103         cout << "_main:" << endl;
104         cout << "        save    %sp,-MINWINDOW,%sp" << endl;
105         this -> block -> emit();
106         cout << "        ret"<< endl;
107         cout << "        restore %o0, 0, %o0" << endl;
108         cout << endl;
109         cout << "        .data" << endl;
110         cout << "#define DW(x)  (((x)+7)&(~0x07))" << endl;
111         cout << "#define MINFRAME ((16+1+6)*4)" << endl;
112         cout << "        MINWINDOW = 96 /* DW(MINFRAME) */" << endl;
113         this -> std_table -> emit();
114         return 0;
115     } else {
116         cerr << "ProgramCls::emit - LOGIC ERROR" << endl;
117         return 0;
118     }
119 }
```

The only data member of *BlockCls* points to the sequence of statements associated with the block. *BlockCls :: emit()* therefore just requests that *stmt_seq* perform its *emit()*.

```
    emit() BlockCls (emit.C)

 92 int BlockCls :: emit() {
 93     //cout << "BlockCls::emit() " << endl;
 94     return this -> stmt_seq -> emit();
 95 }
```

11.7 Producing the Executable

11.7.1 Assembling the Compiler Output

Suppose that *file.p* is the original source file. The assembler file *file.s* is produced by redirecting the compiler's output with a command like the following.

$$epc - c \; file.p > file.s$$

This can then be assembled,

$$cc \; - c \; file.s$$

producing *file.o*.

11.7.2   Linking the Support Functions

Writeln() can be a very simple C function that outputs an integer-valued argument.

```
Writeln() (Writeln.c)

    1    #include <stdio.h>
    2
    3    Writeln(kk) {
    4        printf("     ->%d\n",kk);
    5    }
```

Writeln.o and *file.o* can then be linked into *a.out* by a command like the following.

$$cc\ file.o\ Writeln.o$$

11.8   Makefile

```
emit/Makefile

    1 # Makefile for emitter
    2 PROGRAM:        emit.o
    3
    4 emit.o:         ../p_tree/p_tree.h emit.C
    5        CC -c -g emit.C
    6
    7 clean:
    8        rm -f *.o tmp* a.out
    9
   10 print:
   11        /usr/5bin/pr -n emit.C Makefile > Emit.lst
   12        a2ps Emit.lst | lpr -Pmlw
   13        rm -f Emit.lst
   14
   15 count:
   16        wc *.C Makefile
```

11.9   Suggested Activities

1. Implement your own versions of the various *emit()* functions.

2. Test your *emit()* functions.

    (a) Compile a source program. Assemble and link the output.

    (b) Compare the output of the executable just made with the output from the interpreter.

3. This question requires access to SPARCstation documentation such as the SPARC Architecture Manual [11] or Paul's excellent new text [9].

(a) What is the purpose of the .align pseudo op?

(b) The *sethi* instruction is actually a hardware instruction that has been transcribed to software. Describe this instruction.

(c) Describe the unary operators *%lo* and *%hi*.

4. Modify the code generator module to produce code for another CPU. You may want to choose a simple machine like the early 8080 series, or an available PC CPU.

Appendix A

Program Code

A.1 Main

```
1 /*
2 *      Main.C  -- For Example Compiler
3 */
4
5 #include <iostream.h>
6
7 #include "../ctrl/ctrl.h"
8
9 main(int argc, char** argv) {
10     //cout << " Example Pascal compiler" << endl;
11
12     PControllerCls ctl = new ControllerCls(argc,argv);
13 }
```

A.2 Controller

A.2.1 Definition

```
1 /*
2 *      ctrl.h  Controller definition module
3 */
4
5 typedef class OptionCls *POptionCls;
6 class OptionCls {
7   public:
8         static int option_info();
9         friend class ControllerCls;
10  private:
11        OptionCls();     //Called only by ControllerCls
12        static int     list;
13        static int     emit;
14 };
16
17 class SymtabCls;  // 'forward'
18 class PTreeCls;   //     references
19
20 typedef class ControllerCls *PControllerCls;
```

```
21 class ControllerCls {
22    public:
23         ControllerCls(int argc, char** argv);
24         void          print();
25    private:
26         SymtabCls     *std_table;
27         PTreeCls      *parse_tree;
28         int           open_file(char*);
29 };
```

A.2.2   Implementation

```
 1 /* header */
 2 /*
 3  *       ctrl.C  ControllerCls Implementation Module
 4  */
 5
 6 #include <iostream.h>
 7 #include <stdio.h>
 8 #include <string.h>
 9
10 #include "../scanparse/scanparse.h"
11 #include "../p_tree/p_tree.h"
12 #include "../symtab/symtab.h"
13
14 #include "ctrl.h"
16
17 int OptionCls::list;
18
19 int OptionCls::emit;
20 OptionCls :: OptionCls() {
21     //cout << "OptionCls() " << endl;
22     list = 0;
23     emit = 0;
24 }
25
26 int OptionCls :: option_info() {
27     return (list | emit);
28 }
30 int  ControllerCls :: open_file(char* source_file) {
31     //cout << "ControllerCls::open_file()" << source_file << endl;
32     int length = strlen(source_file);
33     //Check for  .p  extension
34     if ((length > 1) && ((source_file[length -2] == '.') &&
35                           (source_file[length -1] == 'p')  )) {
36         if (!freopen(source_file, "r", stdin)) {
37             cout << "   Cannot open file -- Sorry " << endl;
38             //should be done by an ErrorCls object
39             return 0;
40         } else {
41             return 1;
42         }
43     } else if (length == 0) {
44         cout << "       No file specified" << endl;
45         return 0;
```

```
 46     } else {
 47         cout << "         File must have a  .p  extension" << endl;
 48         //should be done by an ErrorCls object
 49         return 0;
 50     }
 51 }
 53
 54 ControllerCls :: ControllerCls(int argc, char** argv) {
 55     //cout << "ControllerCls() " << endl;
 56
 57
 58     this -> std_table = new SymtabCls;
 59     PScopeCls scp = new ScopeCls;
 60     scp -> vista = this -> std_table;
 61
 62     char *source_file = new char[80];
 63     this -> parse_tree = 0;
 64     if (argc <= 1) {
 65         cout << "         Usage:  epc [-el] <filename>.p" << endl;
 66         return;
 67     } else {
 68         for (int i = 1; i < argc; i++) {
 69             if (*argv[i] == '-') {
 70                 while (*++argv[i]) {
 71                     switch(*argv[i]) {
 72                     case 'l':
 73                         OptionCls :: list = 1;
 74                         continue;
 75
 76                     case 'e':
 77                         OptionCls :: emit = 2;
 78                         continue;
 79
 80                     default:
 81                         cerr << "Unknown option " <<
 82                                         *argv[i] << endl;
 83                     }
 84                 }
 85             } else {
 86             source_file = argv[i];
 87             }
 88         }
 89     }
 90     if (open_file(source_file)) {
 91         ios::sync_with_stdio();
 92         PScanParseCls sp = new ScanParseCls;
 93         this -> parse_tree = sp -> parse_tree;
 94
 95         if (OptionCls::emit) {
 96             parse_tree -> emit();
 97         } else {
 98             parse_tree -> execute();
 99         }
100     }
101 }
```

A.3   Scanner-Parser

A.3.1   Scanner Specification

```
 1 %{
 2 /*
 3  *        scanner.specs
 4  */
 5
 6 #include "y.tab.h"
 7
 8 #include "../ctrl/ctrl.h"
 9 PLexTokCls lex_tok;
10
11 %}
12
13 digit                [0-9]
14 digits               {digit}+
15 letter               [A-Za-z]
16 letter_or_digit      ({letter}|{digit})
17 ident                {letter}{letter_or_digit}*
18 whitespace           [ \t]
19 cr                   [\n]
20 other
21
22 %%
23
24 {whitespace}    {ckout();}
25
26 {cr}            {ckout();}
27
28
29 ";"             {ckout();
30                  lex_tok = new LexTokCls(yylineno, SCTK, 0);
31                  return SCTK;}
32
33 "("             {ckout();
34                  lex_tok = new LexTokCls(yylineno, LPARENTK, 0);
35                  return LPARENTK;}
36
37 ")"             {ckout();
38                  lex_tok = new LexTokCls(yylineno, RPARENTK, 0);
39                  return RPARENTK;}
40
41 ":="            {ckout();
42                  lex_tok = new LexTokCls(yylineno, ASGTK, 0);
43                  return ASGTK;}
44
45 "."             {ckout();
46                  lex_tok = new LexTokCls(yylineno, DOTTK, 0);
47                  return DOTTK;}
48
49 {digits}    {ckout();
50                  lex_tok = new LexTokCls(yylineno, NUMLITERALTK, yytext);
51                  return NUMLITERALTK;}
```

```
52
53 {ident}    {ckout();
54              int actual_tk = ck_reserved_wd();
55              lex_tok = new LexTokCls(yylineno, actual_tk, yytext);
56              return actual_tk;}
57
58 {other}    {ckout();
59              return yytext[0];}
60
61 %%
62
63 #include <string.h>
64 char *textline = new char[257];
65
66 void ckout() {
67     textline = strcat(textline,yytext);
68     if (yytext[0] == '\n') {
69         if (OptionCls::option_info() % 2) {  //List option is a 1
70             cout << "[";
71             cout.width(5);
72             cout <<  yylineno -1 << "]     " << textline ;
73         }
74         textline[0] = '\0';
75     }
76 }
77
78 struct rwtable_str {
79     char *rw_name;      /* lexeme */
80     int  rw_yylex;      /* token  */
81 };
82
83 rwtable_str rwtable[] = {
84     "",                 IDENTIFIERTK,
85     "begin",            BEGINTK,
86     "end",              ENDTK,
87     "program",          PROGRAMTK,
88     "writeln",          WRITETK
89 };
90
91 #define LEN(x)          (sizeof(x)/sizeof((x)[0]))
92 #define ENDTABLE(v)     (v - 1 + LEN(v))
93
94 int ck_reserved_wd() {
95         rwtable_str    *low = rwtable;
96         rwtable_str    *high = ENDTABLE(rwtable);
97         rwtable_str    *mid;
98         int comp;
99         char temp[80];
100
101        strcpy(temp,yytext);
102
103        while (low <= high)
104        {       mid = low + (high-low)/2;
105
106                if ((comp=strcmp(mid->rw_name, temp)) == 0)
```

```
107                        return mid->rw_yylex;
108              else if (comp < 0)
109                        low = mid+1;
110              else
111                        high = mid-1;
112      }
113         return rwtable->rw_yylex;  /* ie. token: IDENTIFIER! */
114 }
115
```

A.3.2 Parser Specification

```
 1 %{
 2 /*
 3  *       parser.gram
 4  */
 5
 6 #define YYSTYPE PPTreeNodeCls
 7 extern char* textline; //Defined in scanner.specs
 8 %}
 9
10 %token PROGRAMTK
11 %token BEGINTK
12 %token ENDTK
13 %token SCTK
14 %token ASGTK
15 %token DOTTK
16 %token IDENTIFIERTK
17 %token NUMLITERALTK
18 %token WRITETK
19 %token LPARENTK
20 %token RPARENTK
21
22 %start Program
23 %%
24
25 Program:
26     PROGRAMTK Identifier SCTK
27     Block
28         {PProgramCls pgm = new ProgramCls($2,$4);}
29     ;
30 Block:
31     BEGINTK
32         StatementSeq
33     ENDTK DOTTK
34         {$$ = new BlockCls($2);}
35     ;
36 StatementSeq:
37     Statement
38         {$$ = new StatementSeqCls($1);}
39     | StatementSeq SCTK Statement
40         {$$ = PStatementSeqCls($1) -> append($3);}
41     ;
42 Statement:
43     /* empty */
```

```
44              {$$ = new EmptyStmtCls;}
45        | AssignmentStmt
46        | WriteStmt
47        ;
48 AssignmentStmt:
49        Identifier ASGTK Expr
50              {$$ = new AssignmentStmtCls($1,$3,textline);}
51        ;
52 WriteStmt:
53        WRITETK LPARENTK Expr RPARENTK
54              {$$ = new WriteStmtCls($3,textline);}
55        ;
56 Expr:
57        Factor
58        ;
59 Factor:
60        Number
61              {$$ = new NumFactorCls($1);}
62        | Identifier
63              {$$ = new VarAccessFactorCls($1);}
64        ;
65 Identifier:
66        IDENTIFIERTK
67              {$$ = new IdentCls();}
68        ;
69 Number:
70        NUMLITERALTK
71              {$$ = new NumLiteralCls();}
72        ;
```

A.3.3 Scanner-Parser Definition

```
 1 /*
 2  *      scanparse.h
 3  */
 4
 5 typedef class LexTokCls *PLexTokCls;
 6 class LexTokCls {
 7   public:
 8        LexTokCls(int LineNo, int Token, char *Lexeme);
 9        char*   get_lexeme() {return lexeme;}
10   private:
11        int     line_no;
12        char    *lexeme;
13        int     token;
14 };
15
16 class ControllerCls;
17 class PTreeCls;
18
19 typedef class ScanParseCls *PScanParseCls;
20 class ScanParseCls {
21   public:
22        ScanParseCls();
23        void        print();
```

```
24        friend class ControllerCls;
25   private:
26        PTreeCls    *parse_tree;
27 };
```

A.3.4   Scanner-Parser Implementation

```
 1
 2 /*
 3  *        scanparse.C
 4  */
 5
 6 //      header
 7 #include <stream.h>
 8 #include "../p_tree/p_tree.h"
 9 #include "scanparse.h"
10 //      end_header
11
12 #include <string.h>
13 LexTokCls :: LexTokCls(int LineNo, int Token, char *Lexeme) {
14     //cout << "LexTokCls(LineNo, Token, Lexeme)" << endl;
15     line_no = LineNo;
16     token   = Token;
17     lexeme = new char[80];
18     if (Lexeme) {
19         strcpy(lexeme,Lexeme);
20     }
21 }
22 //      end_LexTokCls
23
24 PPTreeNodeCls prgm_node; //Global!
25        //Set by top of tree, ProgramCls.
26 #include "scanparse.fct"
27
28 ScanParseCls :: ScanParseCls() {
29     //cout << "ScanParseCls()" << endl;
30     yyparse();
31     parse_tree = new PTreeCls(prgm_node);
32 }
33 //      end_ScanParseCls
```

A.3.5   Scanner Modification for C++

```
 1 /extern char yytext/i\
 2 #include "scanner.h"
 3 s/p, m)/int *p, int m)/
 4 s/int \*p\;//
 5 s/yyoutput(c)/void yyoutput(int c) {/
 6 s/yyunput(c)/void yyunput(int c) {/
 7 /int c\; {/d
 8 s/yyfussy://
 9 $a\
10 #include "scanner.fcts"
```

```
1 int yylook();
2 int yyback(int*,int);
3 void yyless(int);
4 void yyunput(int);
5 int yywrap();
6 void ckout();
7 int ret_token(int);
8 int ck_reserved_wd();
```

A.3.6   Parser Modification for C++

```
1 /define YYERRCODE/a\
2 #include "parser.h"
3 /yynewerror:/d
4 /yyerrlab:/d
5 /++yynerrs;/d
6 $a\
7 #include "parser.fcts"
```

```
1 int yylex();
2 void yyerror(char*);
```

A.4   Symbol Table

A.4.1   Definitions

```
 1 /*
 2 *        symtab.h
 3 */
 4
 5
 6 class ControllerCls;
 7 class SymtabCls;
 8
 9 typedef class ScopeCls *PScopeCls;
10 class ScopeCls {
11    public:
12        ScopeCls()              {;}
13        static SymtabCls        *get_vista() {return vista;}
14        friend class ControllerCls;
15    private:
16        static SymtabCls        *vista;
17 };
18
19 typedef class SymtabEntryCls *PSymtabEntryCls;
20 class SymtabEntryCls    {
21    public:
22        SymtabEntryCls() {;}
23        SymtabEntryCls(char *Name);
24        friend class    SymtabCls;
25        virtual int     emit();
26    protected:
27        char            *name;
```

```
28 };
29
30 typedef class VarAttCls *PVarAttCls;
31 class VarAttCls : public SymtabEntryCls {
32    public:
33          VarAttCls()        {;}
34          VarAttCls(char* Name, int Value);
35          void           set_value(int Value);
36          int            get_value()
37                                {return value;}
38          int            emit();
39    private:
40          int value;
41 };
43
44 /* symtab-def */
45 /* ************************************************************** */
46 /*
47  *        Symbol Table
48  */
49 /* ************************************************************** */
50
51
52 typedef class SymtabCls *PSymtabCls;
53 class SymtabCls  {
54    public:
55          SymtabCls();
56          int            insert(PSymtabEntryCls);
57          PSymtabEntryCls lookup(char*);
58          int            emit();
59    private:
60          int            tablesize;
61          int            next_location;
62          int            *hashtable;
63          PSymtabEntryCls *symtab;  //N.B.:  pointers!
64          int            hash(char *);
65 };
67
```

A.4.2   Symbol Table Implementation

```
1 /*
2  *        symtab.C
3  */
4 #include <iostream.h>
5 #include <string.h>
6
7 #include "symtab.h"
9
10 PSymtabCls ScopeCls::vista; // define static member
11
12 SymtabEntryCls :: SymtabEntryCls(char *Name) {
13    //cout << "SymtabEntryCls()" << endl;
14    name = Name;
15 }
```

```
16
17 int SymtabEntryCls :: emit() {
18     cout << "SymtabEntryCls::emit() BASE CLASS!!!!" << endl;
19     return 0;
20 }
21
22 VarAttCls :: VarAttCls(char *Name, int Value) :
23                                     SymtabEntryCls(Name){
24     //cout << "VarAttCls(Name,Value) " << endl;
25     value = Value;
26 }
27
28 void VarAttCls :: set_value(int Value) {
29     //cout << "VarAttCls::set_value()" << endl;
30     value = Value;
31 }
32
34
35 /* begin-symtab */
36 /* ********************************************************** */
37 /*
38  *      SymtabCls
39  */
40 /* ********************************************************** */
41 SymtabCls :: SymtabCls() {
42     //cout << "SymtabCls::()"<< endl;
43     tablesize = 17;      //Must be a prime for good performance
44     hashtable = new int[tablesize];
45     next_location = 1; // sacrifice 0th spot - hashtable empty:NIL
46     symtab = new PSymtabEntryCls[tablesize]; // Note "P" !!!!
47     PSymtabEntryCls tmp = new SymtabEntryCls("    ");
48     for (int i=0; i<tablesize; i++) {
49         hashtable[i] = 0;
50         symtab[i] = tmp;
51     }
52 }
53
54 int SymtabCls :: hash(char *s) {
55     //cout << "SymtabCls :: hashing for " << s ;
56     char* ss = s;
57     unsigned int h = 0, g;
58     for (; *ss != '\0'; ss++) {
59         h = (h << 4) + *ss;
60         if (g = h & 0xf0000000) {
61             h ^= g >> 24;      // fold top 4 bits onto ------X-
62             h ^= g;            // clear top 4 bits
63         }
64     }
65     //cout << "hashing to " << h % tablesize << endl;
66     return h % tablesize ;
67 }
68
69 int SymtabCls :: insert(PSymtabEntryCls info) {
70     //cout << "SymtabCls::insert()" << endl;
71     //Return 0 if insert successful; else location in symtab.
```

```
72
73     //Look for open slot in the hashtable....
74     int Try, hash_try; //'try' can be a reserved word
75     char *Name = info -> name;
76     //cout<<"preparing to enter"<<Name<<"\n";
77     Try = hash(Name);
78     //cout << "preparing to go into hash table at " << Try << endl;
79
80     while (hash_try = hashtable[Try]) { //something's in hashtable
81         //Check to see if it's the same thing we want to insert...
82         if (!strcmp((symtab[hash_try] -> name), Name)) {
83             return hash_try; //it's already there!
84         } else if (++Try >= tablesize) {
85             //resolve collision by looking for open spot ...
86             Try = 0; //wrap around
87         }
88         //Mature (growing) tables can be at most 2/3 full,
89     }
90     // So an open spot MUST be found
91     hashtable[Try] = next_location;
92     //cout << "entered current loc'n in table " << Try << endl;
93     symtab[next_location++] = info; //Since they're both pointers
94     return 0; // success!
95 }
96
97 PSymtabEntryCls SymtabCls :: lookup(char *Name) {
98     //cout << "SymtabCls :: lookup for " << Name ;
99     int cur_table_size = tablesize;
100    int try, orig_try, hash_try;
101
102    orig_try = try = hash(Name);
103 //cout << "orig_try " << orig_try << "\n";
104    hash_try = hashtable[try];
105 //cout << "hash_try " << hash_try << endl;
106    while (hash_try) {
107        if (!strcmp(symtab[hash_try] -> name, Name)) {
108            return symtab[hash_try];
109        }
110        if (++try >= cur_table_size) try = 0; // wrap around
111        if (try == orig_try) {
112            return symtab[0];
113        } else {
114            hash_try = hashtable[try];
115        }
116 //cout << "hash_try " << hash_try << endl;
117    }
118        return 0; //Failure!
119 }
120
```

A.5   Parse Tree Nodes

A.5.1   Definitions

```
 1 /*
 2 *         p_tree.h
 3 */
 4
 5 class LexTokCls;
 6 class SymtabCls;
 7
 8 typedef class LstSeqBldrCls *PLstSeqBldrCls;
 9 class LstSeqBldrCls {
10   public:
11         LstSeqBldrCls();
12         virtual PLstSeqBldrCls  append(PLstSeqBldrCls);
13         virtual PLstSeqBldrCls  get_next()
14                                 {return next;}
15   private:
16         PLstSeqBldrCls          next;
17 };
19 typedef class PTreeNodeCls *PPTreeNodeCls;
20 class PTreeNodeCls {
21   public:
22         PTreeNodeCls();
23         virtual int           emit();
24         virtual int           execute();
25         virtual void          print();
26         virtual LexTokCls     *get_lex_tok()
27                                 {return lt;}
28   protected:
29         LexTokCls             *lt;
30 };
32 typedef class NumLiteralCls  *PNumLiteralCls;
33 class NumLiteralCls : public PTreeNodeCls {
34   public:
35         NumLiteralCls();
36         int                   get_value()
37                                 {return value;}
38   private:
39         int                   value;
40 };
42 typedef class IdentCls  *PIdentCls;
43 class IdentCls : public PTreeNodeCls {
44   public:
45         IdentCls();
46         char                  *get_name();
47 };
49 typedef class ExprCls  *PExprCls;
50 class ExprCls : public PTreeNodeCls {
51   public:
52         ExprCls();
53         virtual int           evaluate();
54         virtual int           emit();
55   protected:
```

```
56        int value;
57 };
59 typedef class FactorCls *PFactorCls;
60 class FactorCls : public ExprCls {
61   public:
62        FactorCls();
63 };
65 typedef class NumFactorCls *PNumFactorCls;
66 class NumFactorCls : public FactorCls {
67   public:
68        NumFactorCls(PPTreeNodeCls NumLit);
69        int             evaluate();
70        int             emit();
71 };
73
74
75 typedef class VarAccessFactorCls *PVarAccessFactorCls;
76 class VarAccessFactorCls : public FactorCls {
77   public:
78        VarAccessFactorCls(PPTreeNodeCls Ident);
79        int             evaluate();
80        int             emit();
81   private:
82        PPTreeNodeCls ident;
83 };
85 typedef class StatementCls *PStatementCls;
86 class StatementCls : public PTreeNodeCls, public LstSeqBldrCls {
87   public:
88        StatementCls()  {;}
89        StatementCls(char *StmtText);
90        int             emit();
91   protected:
92        char            *stmt_text;
93 };
95
96 typedef class EmptyStmtCls *PEmptyStmtCls;
97 class EmptyStmtCls : public StatementCls {
98   public:
99        EmptyStmtCls()  {;}
100        int             execute();
101        int             emit();
102 };
104 typedef class AssignmentStmtCls *PAssignmentStmtCls;
105 class AssignmentStmtCls : public StatementCls {
106   public:
107        AssignmentStmtCls() {;}
108        AssignmentStmtCls(PPTreeNodeCls Ident,
109                          PPTreeNodeCls Expr,
110                                   char* StmtText);
111        int             execute();
112        int             emit();
113   private:
114        PPTreeNodeCls   ident;          //lhs
115        PPTreeNodeCls   expr;           //rhs
116 };
```

```
118 typedef class WriteStmtCls *PWriteStmtCls;
119 class WriteStmtCls : public StatementCls {
120    public:
121        WriteStmtCls()  {;}
122        WriteStmtCls(PPTreeNodeCls Expr,
123                                  char* StmtText);
124        int             execute();
125        int             emit();
126    private:
127        PPTreeNodeCls   expr;
128 };
130 typedef class StatementSeqCls *PStatementSeqCls;
131 class StatementSeqCls : public PTreeNodeCls {
132    public:
133         StatementSeqCls() {;}
134        StatementSeqCls(PPTreeNodeCls Stmt);
135        int             execute();
136        int             emit();
137        PPTreeNodeCls   append(PPTreeNodeCls);
138    private:
139        StatementCls    *seq_head;
140        StatementCls    *seq_tail;
141 };
143 typedef class BlockCls *PBlockCls;
144 class BlockCls : public PTreeNodeCls {
145    public:
146        BlockCls()       {;}
147        BlockCls(PPTreeNodeCls StmtSeq);
148        int             execute();
149        int             emit();
150    private:
151        PPTreeNodeCls   stmt_seq;
152 };
154 typedef class ProgramCls *PProgramCls;
155 class ProgramCls : public PTreeNodeCls {
156    public:
157        ProgramCls()     {;}
158        ProgramCls(PPTreeNodeCls Ident, PPTreeNodeCls Block);
159        int             execute();
160        int             emit();
161        void            print();
162    private:
163        SymtabCls        *std_table;
164        PIdentCls         ident;
165        PPTreeNodeCls     block;
166 };
168
170 typedef class PTreeCls *PPTreeCls;
171 class PTreeCls {
172    public:
173        PTreeCls(PPTreeNodeCls Root);
174        int             execute();
175        int             emit();
176        void            print();
177    private:
```

```
178          PPTreeNodeCls   root;
179          PPTreeNodeCls   current;
180 };
```

A.5.2   Parse Tree Node Implementation

```
 1 /*
 2  *        p_tree.C
 3  */
 4
 5 #include <iostream.h>
 6 #include <libc.h>
 7 #include <string.h>
 8
 9 #include "../scanparse/scanparse.h"
10 #include "../symtab/symtab.h"
11
12 #include "p_tree.h"
13
14 LstSeqBldrCls :: LstSeqBldrCls() {
15     //cout << "LstSeqBldrCls()" << endl;
16     next = 0;
17 }
18
19 PLstSeqBldrCls LstSeqBldrCls ::
20                     append(PLstSeqBldrCls ToBeAdded) {
21     //cout << "LstSeqBldrCls::append()" << endl;
22     return this -> next = ToBeAdded;
23 }
25 PTreeNodeCls :: PTreeNodeCls() {
26     //cout << "PTreeNodeCls" << endl;
27     extern LexTokCls *lex_tok;
28     lt = lex_tok;
29 }
30
31 int PTreeNodeCls :: emit() {
32     cout << "PTreeNodeCls::emit()  BASECLASS !!!!!!!" << endl;
33     return 0;
34 }
35
36 int PTreeNodeCls :: execute() {
37     cout << "PTreeNodeCls::execute()  BASECLASS !!!!!!!" << endl;
38     return 0;
39 }
40
41 void PTreeNodeCls :: print() {
42     //cout << "PTreeNodeCls::print() " << " lex_tok " << *lt ;
43 }
44
46 NumLiteralCls :: NumLiteralCls() {
47     //cout << "NumLiteralCls" << endl;
48     value = atoi(this -> PTreeNodeCls::lt -> get_lexeme());
49 }
51 IdentCls :: IdentCls() {
52     //cout << "IdentCls" << endl;
```

```
53      char *name = this -> PTreeNodeCls::lt -> get_lexeme();
54
55      PSymtabCls scp = ScopeCls::get_vista();
56      PSymtabEntryCls found_it = scp -> lookup(name);
57      if (!found_it) {
58          PVarAttCls va = new VarAttCls(name,0);
59          scp -> insert(va);
60      }
61 }
62
63 char *IdentCls :: get_name() {
64      //cout << "IdentCls::get_name()" << endl;
65      return this -> PTreeNodeCls::lt -> get_lexeme();
66 }
68 ExprCls :: ExprCls() {
69      //cout << "ExprCls" << endl;
70 }
71
72 int ExprCls :: evaluate() {
73      cout << "ExprCls::evaluate()  BASE CLASS !!!!!!!" << endl;
74      return 0;
75 }
76
77 int ExprCls :: emit() {
78      cout << "ExprCls::emit()  BASE CLASS !!!!!!!" << endl;
79      return 0;
80 }
81
82 FactorCls :: FactorCls() {
83      //cout << "FactorCls() " << endl;
84 }
86 NumFactorCls :: NumFactorCls(PPTreeNodeCls NumLit) {
87      //cout << "NumFactorCls() " << endl;
88      if (!NumLit) {
89          cerr << "NumFactorCls - LOGIC ERROR" << endl;
90      }
91      ExprCls::value = PNumLiteralCls(NumLit) -> get_value();
92      //cout << " value " << ExprCls::value << endl;
93 }
94
95 int NumFactorCls :: evaluate() {
96      //cout << "NumFactorCls::evaluate()" << endl;
97      return ExprCls::value;
98 }
99
100 VarAccessFactorCls :: VarAccessFactorCls(PPTreeNodeCls Ident) {
101      //cout << "VarAccessFactorCls() " << endl;
102      if (!Ident) {
103          cerr << "VarAccessFactorCls() - LOGIC ERROR" << endl;
104      }
105      ident = Ident;
106      char *name = PIdentCls(ident) -> get_name();
107      PSymtabCls scp = ScopeCls::get_vista();
108      PSymtabEntryCls found_it = scp -> lookup(name);
109      if (!found_it) {
```

```
110         cerr << "        " << *name << " used but not set" << endl;
111         PVarAttCls va = new VarAttCls(name,0);
112         scp -> insert(va);
113         ExprCls::value = 0;
114     } else {
115         ExprCls::value = PVarAttCls(found_it) -> get_value();
116     }
117 }
118
119 int VarAccessFactorCls :: evaluate() {
120     //cout << "VarAccessFactorCls::evaluate()" << endl;
121     char *name = PIdentCls(ident) -> get_name();
122     PSymtabCls scp = ScopeCls::get_vista();
123     PSymtabEntryCls found_it = scp -> lookup(name);
124     return  PVarAttCls(found_it) -> get_value();
125 }
127
128 StatementCls :: StatementCls(char *StmtText) {
129     //cout << "StatementCls()" << endl;
130     stmt_text = new char[strlen(StmtText)+1];
131     strcpy(stmt_text,StmtText);
132 }
133
134 AssignmentStmtCls :: AssignmentStmtCls(
135                     PPTreeNodeCls Ident,
136                     PPTreeNodeCls Expr,
137                         char* TextLine):
138                             StatementCls(TextLine) {
139     //cout << "AssignmentStmtCls() " << endl;
140     if (!Ident || !Expr) {
141         cerr << "AssignmentStmtCls() - LOGIC ERROR " << endl;
142     }
143     ident = Ident;
144     expr = Expr;
145 }
146
147 WriteStmtCls :: WriteStmtCls(PPTreeNodeCls Expr,
148                         char* TextLine):
149                             StatementCls(TextLine) {
150     //cout << "WriteStmtCls() " << endl;
151     if (!Expr) {
152         cerr << "WriteStmtCls() - LOGIC ERROR " << endl;
153     }
154     expr = Expr;
155 }
157
158 StatementSeqCls :: StatementSeqCls (PPTreeNodeCls Stmt) {
159     //cout << "StatementSeqCls() " << endl;
160     seq_tail = seq_head = PStatementCls(Stmt);
161 }
162
163 PPTreeNodeCls StatementSeqCls :: append(PPTreeNodeCls Stmt) {
164     //cout << "StatementSeqCls::append()" << endl;
165     if (!seq_tail) {
166         cerr << "StatementSeqCls::append() -- LOGIC ERROR" << endl;
```

```
167     } else {
168         seq_tail = PStatementCls(seq_tail ->
169                     LstSeqBldrCls::append(PStatementCls(Stmt)));
170     }
171     return this;
172 }
174
175 BlockCls :: BlockCls(PPTreeNodeCls StmtSeq) {
176     //cout << "BlockCls" << endl;
177     stmt_seq = StmtSeq;
178 }
180
181 extern PPTreeNodeCls prgm_node; //declared in scanparse.C
182 ProgramCls :: ProgramCls(PPTreeNodeCls Ident, PPTreeNodeCls Block) {
183     //cout << "ProgramCls() " << endl;
184     ident = PIdentCls(Ident);
185     block = PBlockCls(Block);
186     std_table = ScopeCls::get_vista();
187     prgm_node = this;
188 }
189
190 void ProgramCls::print() {
191     cout << "ProgramCls::print()" << endl;
192 }
194
196
197 PTreeCls :: PTreeCls(PPTreeNodeCls Root) {
198     //cout << "PTreeCls()" << endl;
199     root = current = Root;
200 }
201
202 void PTreeCls :: print() {
203     cout << "PTreeCls " << endl;
204     root -> print();
205 }
```

A.5.3 Parse Tree Node Interpreter Functions

```
1 /*
2  *      interp.C
3  */
4
5 #include <iostream.h>
6
7 #include "../p_tree/p_tree.h"
8 #include "../symtab/symtab.h"
9
10 int EmptyStmtCls :: execute() {
11     //cout << "EmptyStmtCls::execute()" << endl;
12     return 0;
13 }
14
15 int AssignmentStmtCls :: execute() {
16     //cout << "AssignmentStmtCls::execute() " << endl;
17     int rval = PExprCls(expr) -> evaluate();
```

```
18
19      char *name = PIdentCls(ident) -> get_name();
20      PSymtabCls scp = ScopeCls::get_vista();
21      PSymtabEntryCls found_it = scp -> lookup(name);
22      if (!found_it) {
23          cout << "AssignmentStmtCls::execute() LOGIC ERROR" << endl;
24          //should be done with an ErrorCls object
25      } else {
26          PVarAttCls(found_it) -> set_value(rval);
27      }
28      return 0;
29 }
30
31 int WriteStmtCls :: execute() {
32      //cout << "WriteStmtCls::execute() " << expr << endl;
33      cout << "  -> " << PExprCls(expr) -> evaluate() << endl;
34      return 0;
35 }
36
37 int StatementSeqCls :: execute() {
38      //cout << "StatementSeqCls::execute() " << endl;
39      PPTreeNodeCls p = this -> seq_head;
40      while (p) {
41          p -> execute();
42          p = PStatementCls(PStatementCls(p) -> get_next());
43      }
44      return 0;
45 }
46
47 int BlockCls :: execute() {
48      //cout << "BlockCls::execute() " << endl;
49      return this -> stmt_seq -> execute();
50 }
51
52 int ProgramCls :: execute() {
53      //cout << "ProgramCls::execute() " << endl;
54      return this -> block -> execute();
55 }
56
57 int PTreeCls :: execute() {
58      //cout << "PTreeCls::execute() " << endl;
59      if (!root) {
60          cerr << "PTreeCls::execute - LOGIC ERROR" << endl;
61          return 0;
62      } else {
63          return root -> execute();
64      }
65 }
66
```

A.5.4   Parse Tree Node Emitter Functions

```
1 /*
2 *       emit.C
3 */
```

```
4
5 #include <iostream.h>
6
7 #include "../symtab/symtab.h"
8
9 int VarAttCls :: emit() {
10     //cout << "VarAttCls::emit()" << endl;
11     cout << "    .align  4" << endl;
12     cout << "    .common _" << SymtabEntryCls::name;
13     cout << ",4" << endl;
14     return 0;
15 }
16
17 int SymtabCls :: emit() {
18     //cout << "SymtabCls::emit()" << endl;
19
20     cout << "    .bss" << endl;
21     //First (i=1) SymtabEntryCls object is for program name
22     for (int i=2; i < next_location; i++) {
23         symtab[i] -> emit();
24     }
25     return 0;
26 }
27
28 #include "../p_tree/p_tree.h"
29
30 int NumFactorCls :: emit() {
31     //cout << "NumFactorCls::emit()" << endl;
32     cout << "    mov     0x" << hex <<
33                     ExprCls::value << ",%o0" << endl;
34     return 0;
35 }
36 int VarAccessFactorCls :: emit() {
37     //cout << "VarAccessFactorCls::emit()" << endl;
38     char *ident_str = PIdentCls(ident) -> get_name();
39     cout << "    sethi   %hi(_" ;
40         cout << ident_str;
41         cout << "),%o0" << endl;
42     cout << "    ld      [%o0+%lo(_" ;
43         cout << ident_str;
44         cout << ")],%o0" << endl;
45     return 0;
46 }
47
48 int StatementCls :: emit() {
49     cout << "! " << stmt_text << endl;
50     return 0;
51 }
52
53 int EmptyStmtCls :: emit() {
54     //cout << "EmptyStmtCls::emit()" << endl;
55     return 0;
56 }
57
58 int AssignmentStmtCls :: emit() {
```

```
59      //cout << "AssignmentStmtCls::emit()" << endl;
60      StatementCls::emit();
61      expr -> emit();
62
63      char *ident_str = PIdentCls(ident) -> get_name();
64      cout << "    sethi   %hi(_" ;
65          cout << ident_str;
66          cout << "),%o1" << endl;
67      cout << "    st      %o0,[%o1+%lo(_";
68          cout << ident_str;
69          cout << ")]" << endl;
70      return 0;
71 }
72
73 int WriteStmtCls :: emit() {
74      //cout << "WriteStmtCls::emit()" << endl;
75      StatementCls::emit();
76      expr -> emit();
77      cout << "    call    _Writeln,1" << endl;
78      cout << "    nop" << endl;
79      return 0;
80 }
81
82 int StatementSeqCls :: emit() {
83      //cout << "StatementSeqCls::emit() " << endl;
84      PPTreeNodeCls p = this -> seq_head;
85      while (p) {
86          p -> emit();
87          p = PStatementCls(PStatementCls(p) -> get_next());
88      }
89      return 0;
90 }
91
92 int BlockCls :: emit() {
93      //cout << "BlockCls::emit() " << endl;
94      return this -> stmt_seq -> emit();
95 }
96
97 int ProgramCls :: emit() {
98      //cout << "ProgramCls::emit() " << endl;
99      if (block && std_table) {
100         cout << "        .text" << endl;
101         cout << "        .global _main" << endl << endl;
102
103         cout << "_main:" << endl;
104         cout << "        save    %sp,-MINWINDOW,%sp" << endl;
105         this -> block -> emit();
106         cout << "        ret"<< endl;
107         cout << "        restore %o0, 0, %o0" << endl;
108         cout << endl;
109         cout << "        .data" << endl;
110         cout << "#define DW(x)   (((x)+7)&(~0x07))" << endl;
111         cout << "#define MINFRAME ((16+1+6)*4)" << endl;
112         cout << "        MINWINDOW = 96 /* DW(MINFRAME) */" << endl;
113         this -> std_table -> emit();
```

```
114        return 0;
115     } else {
116        cerr << "ProgramCls::emit - LOGIC ERROR" << endl;
117        return 0;
118     }
119 }
120
121 int PTreeCls :: emit() {
122    //cout << "PTreeCls::emit() " << endl;
123    if (! root) {
124        cerr << "PTreeCls::emit - LOGIC ERROR" << endl;
125        return 0;
126    } else {
127        return root -> emit();
128    }
129 }
130
```

Appendix B

Answers to Activities

B.1 Chapter 1 Activities

Evaluate your development platform by completing a system configuration table.

> Getting specific information about your hardware can be surprisingly time-consuming, especially if you have a workstation. Unfortunately, system documentation is often overly general so that it can be used for an entire family of configurations. However, you may find that sales representatives will give you reliable system information from your written purchase agreement.

B.2 Chapter 2 Activities

1. (Experiment with C++.)

   (a) Write a C++ program that outputs the following message.

   Hello world!

   ```
   #include <stream.h>

   main() {
       cout << "Hello world" << endl;
   }
   ```

   (b) Write a C++ function to read characters from stdin and produce a tally of:

   i. The number of white spaces.

   ii. The number of non white space characters.

```
#include <iostream.h>

void Counter(int * white, int * text) {
   int lineCnt=0;
   char ch;

   while( cin.get(ch)) {
      switch (ch) {
         case '\t':              // tab
         case ' ':               // space
         case '\f':              // formfeed
         case '\r':              // carriage return
            (*white)++;
            break;
         case '\n':
            lineCnt++;
            (*white)++;
            break;
         default:
            ++(*text);
            break;
      }
   }
   return;
}
```

(c) Write a C++ main program that calls the function in the above exercise. Test it on a number of different kinds of input.

```
#include <iostream.h>

extern void Counter(int*, int*);

main() {
   int charCnt = 0, whiteCnt = 0;
   Counter(&whiteCnt, &charCnt);
   cout << whiteCnt << "WhiteSpaces" << endl;
   cout << charCnt << "Non-WhiteSpace Characters";
   cout << endl;
}
```

(d) (A useful class for possible future application.)

Write a C++ definition and implementation for *StringCls*, a class that abstracts the notion of strings. Be sure to include members for data storage, a constructor that converts the usual (char*) C++ string to *StringCls* and some means for a *StringCls* object to output itself.

```
typedef char *Pchar;

typedef class StringCls *PStringCls;
class StringCls {
   public:
        StringCls(Pchar s);
        void            print();
   private:
        struct str_rep {
                Pchar str;
                int n;
        };
        str_rep *p;
};
```

```
#include <iostream.h>
#include <string.h>
#include <libc.h>

#include "str.h"

StringCls :: StringCls(Pchar s) {
    p = new str_rep;
    p -> str = new char[ strlen(s) + 1];
    strcpy(p->str,s);
    p -> n = 1;
}


void StringCls :: print() {
    if (strlen(p->str) == 0) {
        cout << "''";
    } else {
        cout << "'";
        cout << p->str;
        cout << "'";
    }
}
```

```
#include "str.h"

main() {
    PStringCls st_ptr = new StringCls("testing");
    st_ptr -> print();
}
```

2. (Classes: Encapsulation)

Let's imagine that we have to work with two C functions *function1()* and *function2()* that communicate via a global variable *glbl*. It is not too difficult to think of situations where we would like to avoid using such globals, but would not want to or even be able to rewrite the two functions. However, it is possible to use the notion of a class to encapsulate the global and the functions.

(a) (Definition of C++ classes) Define a class *EncapsCls* that has a public constructor an the following three private members.

- An integer variable *glbl*.

- A void function *function1()*.

- A void function *function2()*.

Place your definition the class definition file *encaps.h*.

```
typedef class EncapsCls *PEncapsCls;
class EncapsCls {
    public:
        EncapsCls();
    private:
        int     glbl;
        void    function1();
        void    function2();
};
```

(b) (Implementation of C++ classes) Place the following information in the corresponding implementation file *encaps.C*

- Preprocessor **include** commands for *stream* and *encaps.h*.

- *EncapsCls* constructor implementation. Have this function contain an initialization of *glbl* and then the two calls to the functions previously contained in *main()*.

- *EncapsCls :: function1()* implementation.

- *EncapsCls :: function2()* implementation.

```
#include <iostream.h>

#include "encaps.h"

EncapsCls :: EncapsCls() {
    cout << "EncapsCls() " << endl;
    glbl = 12345;
    function1();
    function2();
}

void EncapsCls :: function1() {
    cout << "EncapsCls::function1" << endl;
}

void EncapsCls :: function2() {
    cout << "EncapsCls::function2" << endl;
}
```

(c) (Main module) Write an appropriate *main()* that creates an *EncapsCls*
object. Place this in a separate main module, *main.C*.

```
#include "encaps.h"

main() {
    PEncapsCls ec = new EncapsCls;
}
```

(d) (Separate compilation)

    i. Only compile *main()*, suppressing the linking by using the *-c* option
as follows.

```
CC -c main.C
```

    ii. Compile the encapulator module, again with a command something
like the following.

```
CC -c encaps.C
```

    iii. Link the object files *main.o* and *encaps.o*.

```
CC  main.o encaps.o
```

    iv. Test the execution of the system.

3. (Classes: Derivation) One possible extension of the example compiler is to
add error detection and reporting capabilities. It turns out that the detection
can be easily accomplished by slightly modifying the existing classes. We
therefore only need to design and implement objects that can be used to
report the errors to the user.

(a) Analysis.

- Make a list of the various kinds of messages you will want to send to the user. Be sure to also consider warning messages.

> – Warning
> – Error (during compilation)
> – Run-time Error.

- Are there any common features or behaviors of the system for the various messages?

> – All of them send a message to user.
> – Class should encapsulate total number of errors.

- What are the features or behaviors of the system that are unique to each kind of message?

> – Warning
>   Should just print out message.
> – Error (during compilation)
>   Should print out message and then increment number of errors so that compilation may terminate after a reasonable error threshold has been reached.
> – Run-time Error.
>   Should print out message and then terminate the interpreting or execution of the program.

(b) Design.

- Define *MessageCls*, a class encapsulating any data or behavior members that are common to all the various errors and warnings. Be sure to include some form of printing behavior.

```
typedef char *PChar;

typedef class MessageCls *PMessageCls;
class MessageCls {
    public:
        MessageCls();
        virtual void notify(PChar) {;}
    protected:
        static int      num_errors;
        void            send_message(PChar);
};
```

- Define the various kinds of error and warning classes by deriving them from *MessageCls*. Consider making the *MessageCls* print behavior virtual and then redefining it for the derived classes as may be necessary. What happens if you do not make the base class print behavior a virtual function but include print behaviors for the derived classes?

```
class MessageCls; //declaration

typedef class WarningCls *PWarningCls;
class WarningCls : public MessageCls {
    public:
        WarningCls() {;}
        void notify(PChar);
};

typedef class ErrorCls *PErrorCls;
class ErrorCls : public MessageCls {
    public:
        ErrorCls() {;}
        void notify(PChar);
};

typedef class RunTimeErrorCls *PRunTimeErrorCls;
class RunTimeErrorCls : public MessageCls {
    public:
        RunTimeErrorCls() {;}
        void notify(PChar);
};
```

(c) Implementation.

   i. Implement the constructor(s) and behaviors for *MessageCls*.

```
#include <iostream.h>

#include "message.h"

MessageCls :: MessageCls() {
    cout << "MessageCls" << endl;
}

void MessageCls :: send_message(PChar Mesg) {
    cerr << Mesg << endl;
}
```

  ii. Implement the various error and warning classes.

```
#include <iostream.h>
#include <libc.h> //for exit()

#include "message.h"
#include "error.h"

void WarningCls :: notify(PChar Mesg) {
    cerr << endl << "Warning: " ;
    MessageCls :: send_message(Mesg);
}

void ErrorCls :: notify(PChar Mesg) {
    cerr << endl << "Compile-time Error: " ;
    MessageCls :: send_message(Mesg);
    MessageCls :: num_errors++;
}

void RunTimeErrorCls :: notify(PChar Mesg) {
    cerr << endl << "RunTimeError: " ;
    MessageCls :: send_message(Mesg);
    cerr << "Terminating session -- sorry" << endl;
    exit(1);
}
```

iii.   • Carefully test the various member functions.

   • Test the derived classes Perhaps it would be best to implement
     and test one derived class at a time. Be especially careful to note
     the order of execution of the derived and the base constructors.
     Also verify that the print behaviors of the derived classes are
     exactly what you have in mind. In particular, take whatever
     steps are necessary to insure that the base class print behavior
     is not being used if it should not be.

   | Add a BASE CLASS message, or declare pure virtual. |

4. (Classes: Late Binding)

For sake of discussion, let's say that *Derived1Cls* and *Derived2Cls* are two of
the error or warning classes derived in Activity 3, above, which have print
behaviors sufficiently different that they can be distinguished. Make a test
program that does the following.

(a) Contains a variable *base_ptr* of *MessageCls* * type.

(b) Creates *Derived1Cls* and *Derived2Cls* objects in free store (i.e., on the
    heap).

(c) Places a pointer to the *Derived1Cls* object in *base_ptr* and then executes
    the objects print behavior using something like the following command.

$$base\_ptr-> print()$$

(d) Also places a pointer to the *Derived2Cls* object in *base_ptr* and executes its print behavior by issuing exactly the same command.

```
#include <iostream.h>

#include "message.h"
#include "error.h"

main() {
    PMessageCls base_ptr;

    base_ptr  = new WarningCls;
    base_ptr -> notify("This is only a warning");

    base_ptr  = new ErrorCls;
    base_ptr -> notify("Bad syntax");

    base_ptr  = new RunTimeErrorCls;
    base_ptr -> notify("array out of bounds");

    cout << "note what happens to this" << endl;
}
```

B.3 Chapter 3 Activities

1. It may be helpful to explore the capabilities of an existing compiler before you begin the analysis and design of your own system. This question is designed to raise a number of issues for your consideration.

   Locate an existing compiler and corresponding documentation on your system.

   (a) Most compilers have an option displaying the highest level compilation commands used during a normal session. On many compilers this is a - *dryrun* switch. Using this feature, make a list of the sequence of activities normally performed by your compiler.

   Consider the following program.

```
program sample;
begin
    writeln(123)
end.
```

   Dryrun on my system produces the following output.

```
First, execute the preprocessor ...
/usr/lang/SC1.0/cpp -undef -Dunix -Dsun -Dsparc -I/usr/lang\
/SC1.0/include f.p >/tmp/cpp.01266.0.pi

Then a first pass using program pc0 ...
/usr/lang/SC1.0/pc0 /tmp/pc0.01266.1.s -o /tmp/pc0.01266.2.ir\
/tmp/cpp.01266.0.pi

Remove the temporary file ...
rm /tmp/cpp.01266.0.pi

Produce symbol table information for run-time system ...
/usr/lang/SC1.0/cg -cg87 /tmp/pc0.01266.2.ir >/tmp/cg.01266.3.s

Remove the temporary file ...
rm /tmp/pc0.01266.2.ir

Assemble the code ...
/usr/lang/SC1.0/as -o f.o -Q -cg87 /tmp/pc0.01266.1.s\
/tmp/cg.01266.3.s
rm /tmp/pc0.01266.1.s

Prepare for link-editing ...
/usr/lang/SC1.0/pc3 /usr/lang/SC1.0/pcexterns.o f.o

Perform the link-editing ...
/bin/ld -dc -dp -e start -X -o a.out /usr/lang/SC1.0/crt0.o \
/usr/lang/SC1.0/cg87/_crt1.o -L/usr/lang/SC1.0/cg87 \
-L/usr/lang/SC1.0 f.o -lpc -lm -lc

Final cleanup ...
rm /tmp/cg.01266.3.s
rm f.o
```

(b) Is your compiler a multi-pass compiler? If so, what tasks are performed
    on each pass? It may be possible to 'watch' this by putting a compiling
    job in the back ground and then running a system-watch program. If
    so, approximately how much time does each pass take?

> Clearly the amount of time depends on the size of the source
> program. My system spends approximately a tenth of the total
> compile time in the various passes of the compiler and the
> remainder in the assembler and linker/loader.

(c) Does your compiler have an optimizer? Write a simple program that
    is fairly compute-bound, e.g., nested iterations executing a selection
    statement. Compare the performance of regularly compiled code with
    that which as been optimized.

    Consider the following pascal program.

```
program slow;
const
    N = 1000000;
var
    i,j: integer;
begin
    for i := 1 to N do begin
        j := trunc(2.0*N);
        if (2*i = N/2) then writeln(i)
    end
end.
```

Compiling normally, executing, compiling with one of the 'normal' optimization levels, and then executing produces the following output.

```
% /bin/time a.out
    250000
            3.8 real          3.3 user          0.2 sys
% pc -O slow.p
% /bin/time a.out
    250000
            2.4 real          1.9 user          0.3 sys
pegasus%
```

The first number represents the number of seconds during the entire execution, the second is the actual time the program or library code is being executed, and the third is the time spent executing system calls.

It's interesting that this level of optimization is not removing invariant expressions! You can see that by optimizing the following program

```
program slow;
const        ·
    N = 1000000;
var
    i,j: integer;
begin
    for i := 1 to N do begin
        {j := trunc(2.0*N);}
        if (2*i = N/2) then writeln(i)
    end
end.
```

and then noting the following execution information.

```
% /bin/time a.out
    250000
            2.2 real          1.6 user          0.2 sys
%
```

(d) Scan the list of compiler options and make a list of those you would like
to include in your compiler. In particular, what kind of print options
are important?

> This activity is really designed to give you a place to
> raise questions. Spending time discussing the purpose of
> the various options has helped provide perspective on the
> overall task and structure of compilers.

(e) Place an intentional error in a source program.

How are lexical errors reported? There are two lexical errors in the
following program.

```
program lex_err;
begin
    writeln(12w3)
end.
```

My system reports these lexical errors as violating the original standard
(the s) as follows.

```
      1   program lex_err;
s --------------^--- '_' in an identifier is nonstandard
      3         writeln(12w3)
s -------------------^--- Space required between
                             number and word-symbol
s 3 - Illegal format
```

How are syntax errors indicated?

> A lower case 'e' or upper case 'E' is used.

Leaving out the **begin** in the following program

```
program syntaxerr;
    writeln(123)
end.
```

produces the following output.

```
Thu Jun 30 13:02:58 1994   syntaxerr.p:
      2         writeln(123)
E ----------^--- Malformed declaration
      3   end.
E ------^--- Malformed declaration
E ------^--- Unrecoverable syntax error - QUIT
Compilation failed
```

Incidentally, fixing this syntax error

```
program syntaxerr;
begin
    writeln(123)
end.
```

then allows compiler to find the following static semantic error.

```
Thu Jun 30 13:13:34 1994  semanticerr.p:
e 4 - Output is used but not defined in the
                         program statement
```

(f) Is there an interpreter available? How is it used? Compare time performance of interpreted programs with compiled programs.

```
The absence of such a system was one of the motivations
for building the example compiler.
```

(g) A pretty printer reformats the source program, based upon the syntax of the source program and subject to various style options. Pretty printers can be implemented as a part of the compiler system or as a separate program.

   i. Pretty print a number of language constructs: iteration statements, control statements, subprogram declarations, etc.
   The following program

```
program noindent;
var i:integer;x:real;
function even(i:integer):boolean;
begin even := not odd(i) end;
begin
for i:=1 to 100 do begin if
even(i) then writeln(i div 2) end end.
```

is replaced by the following formatted one.

```
program noindent;
var
    i: integer;
    x: real;
function even(i: integer): boolean;
begin
    even := not odd(i)
end; { even }

begin
    for i := 1 to 100 do begin
        if even(i) then
            writeln(i div 2)
    end
end. { noindent }
```

    ii. What formatting options are available?

> - Fully parenthesize expressions.
> - Map all identifiers and keywords to lower case.
> - Strip comments from the input text.
> - Underline keywords

(h) What kind of debugging aids does your compiler provide?

    i. What options are possible for range checking of array indices?

    ii. Use the system debugger to trace a simple program.

    iii. A profiler counts the number of times that certain subprograms or structures are executed. Profile a simple program containing multiple calls to a particular subprogram.

> These system-specific questions are designed to encourage reading of system documentation. You should be thinking about how a compiler has to be designed to interface with other system utilities such as debuggers and profilers.

2. Prepare a simple analysis document for your own compiler:

(a) Write a description of the system you would like to build. Include possible extensions to the description in this chapter. Adding a looping statement or an additional data type are excellent projects.

(b) Make a list of important objects and classes for your compiler.

(c) Specify the format for input to your compiler. Do the same for compiler output.

> You might start by making slight modifications of the specifications and lists given in the project book.

3. Design and build a directory structure suitable for your own version of the compiler. You may want to do this incrementally, adding subdirectories only as needed.

Students usually settle on a structure similar to the following.

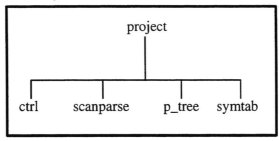

4. Construct a makefile for the outer level directory that calls corresponding makefiles for each of the subdirectories.

```
# Makefile for typical student directory

SUBDIR  =        ctrl scanparse p_tree symtab

PROGRAM:
                 for i in ${SUBDIR}; do \
                         (echo " "; echo $$i;cd $$i; make;); \
                 done
                 CC -o epc -g $(DOTOHS)
```

B.4   Chapter 4 Activities

1. Implement your own version of *main()*. If you have not yet worked on the *ctrl* module, comment out any reference to *ControllerCls*.

> Many of us have already adopted the use of stubs as presented in early programming classes. Of course, that's a technique where the subprogram call is complete and the subprogram is not.
>
> Object-oriented programming often is simpler with reverse situation: an 'incomplete' call at least until the corresponding class constructor is implemented. The suggestion of commenting out the call has not been entirely satisfactory, since we often forget where the call was placed. One person began an excellent practice of placing the actual call in an output statement also containing code location information. This provided a visual reminder to 'turn on' the calling code as soon as the class implementation was sufficiently complete.

2. If your operating system supports command line communication,

(a) Experiment with the program *main()* from Activity 1 by:

- Adding instructions to *main()* that will print out the values of *argc*, **argv* and ***argv*.

```
#include <iostream.h>
#include <string.h>

main(int argc, char** argv) {
    cout << "Experimenting with command line args" << endl;
    cout << "    argc: " << argc << endl;
    for (int i=0; i < argc; i++) {
        cout << "                    i: " << i << endl;
        cout << "    length(argv[i]): " << strlen(argv[i]) << endl;
        cout << "             argv[i]: " << argv[i] << endl;
    }
}
```

- Executing main with no extra command line arguments. Note the value of *argc* and *argv*.

```
% a.out
Experimenting with command line args
argc: 1
                i: 0
    length(argv[i]): 5
          argv[i]: a.out

%
```

Then repeat with first one and then several arguments.

```
%a.out with command line arguments
Experimenting with command line args
argc: 5
                i: 0
   length(argv[i]): 5
           argv[i]: a.out
                i: 1
   length(argv[i]): 4
           argv[i]: with
                i: 2
   length(argv[i]): 7
           argv[i]: command
                i: 3
   length(argv[i]): 4
           argv[i]: line
                i: 4
   length(argv[i]): 9
           argv[i]: arguments

% a.out 1 2 3 4 5 6
Experimenting with command line args
argc: 7
                i: 0
   length(argv[i]): 5
           argv[i]: a.out
                i: 1
   length(argv[i]): 1
           argv[i]: 1
                i: 2
   length(argv[i]): 1
           argv[i]: 2
                i: 3
   length(argv[i]): 1
           argv[i]: 3
                i: 4
   length(argv[i]): 1
           argv[i]: 4
                i: 5
   length(argv[i]): 1
           argv[i]: 5
                i: 6
   length(argv[i]): 1
           argv[i]: 6
```

(b) Write a C++ program that prints out the sum of any string of integers input through the command line.

```
#include <iostream.h>
#include <libc.h>  // for atoi
#include <ctype.h> // for isdigit

int isnumeric(char* str) {
    int tst = 0;
    while (*str && (tst = isdigit(*str++))) ;
    return (tst);
}

main(int argc, char** argv) {
    int sum=0;
    cout << "Summing integers in command line" << endl;
    for (int i=1; i < argc; i++) {
        if (isnumeric(argv[i])) {
            sum += atoi(argv[i]);
        }
    }
    cout << "   Sum: " << sum << endl;
}
```

The above program produces the following output.

```
% a.out 1 2.3 4
Summing integers in command line
Sum: 5

% a.out 123 2b4 345 abc
Summing integers in command line
Sum: 468

% a.out
Summing integers in command line
Sum: 0
```

B.5   Chapter 5 Activities

1. Implement your own versions of *ctrl.h* and *ctrl.C*. Again, you will want to comment out any references to classes which have not yet been defined or implemented. You will have arrived at the first execution milestone when you complete the coding and testing of the various classes in this module.

> I usually spend some class time talking about C++ I/O. Students are often willing to accept *ios::sync_with_stdio();* on faith, but eventually that approach leads to insufficient understanding of important ideas. Appendix A in Lippman [8] as well as Chapter 3 of the C++ version 2.0 release notes have helpful discussions of these ideas.
>
> I'm not totally pleased with the indicated method of redirecting the source file to standard input and would greatly appreciate any solution you might have that uses *iostream* exclusively.

2. The content of a *.h* (include) file is always a matter requiring some discussion or even debate. Question: Why not put all the messy header information contained in the *ctrl.C* header section into the *ctrl.h* and then import it into *ctrl.C* with the single line *#include"ctrl.h"*?

> C++'s Stroustrup [12, Page 22] discusses both the purpose and the problems of header files. He cites consistency between source files as the purpose, and replication of declarations as the major problem. It is not too hard to produce multiple class definition problems by placing includes inside a 'dot.h' file.
>
> Lippman [8, Page 13] suggests the use of conditional directives to guard against multiple processing of a header file. While some people do master this, I have found that a general *no variable definitions and no other includes* include policy to be an easier concept for them. See Lippman [8, Pages 173–174] for additional discussion of header file design.

3. (Possible Extension)

   (a) Modify the definition of *OptionCls* to include a run-time semantic check option *-C*.

   (b) Make the corresponding modifications to the *OptionCls* implementation code to provide for the new option.

   (c) Make modifications to the *ControllerCls* constructor so that the option is detected and the corresponding option value is set.

   (d) Make modifications to *AssignmentStmt* behavior so that the option affects the behavior of the compiler.

```
typedef class OptionCls *POptionCls;
class OptionCls {
    public:
        static int option_info();
        friend class ControllerCls;
    private:
        OptionCls();        //Called only by ControllerCls
        static int      list;
        static int      emit;
        static int      sem_chk;
};
```

```
OptionCls :: OptionCls() {
    //cout << "OptionCls() " << endl;
    list = 0;
    emit = 0;
    sem_chk = 0;
}

int OptionCls :: option_info() {
    return (list | emit | sem_chk);
}

ControllerCls :: ControllerCls(int argc, char** argv) {
    // ....
    } else {
        for (int i = 1; i < argc; i++) {
            if (*argv[i] == '-') {
                while (*++argv[i]) {
                    switch(*argv[i]) {
                    case 'l':
                        OptionCls :: list = 1;
                        continue;
                    case 'e':
                        OptionCls :: emit = 2;
                        continue;
                    case 'C':
                        OptionCls :: sem_chk = 4;
                        continue;
                    default:
                        cerr << "Unknown option " <<
                                        *argv[i] << endl;
                    }
                }
            } else {
                source_file = argv[i];
            }
        }
    }
```

```
#include <iostream.h>
#include <libc.h>

#include "../ctrl/ctrl.h"
#include "../p_tree/p_tree.h"
#include "../symtab/symtab.h"
#include "../consts/consts.h"

int AssignmentStmtCls :: execute() {
    //cout << "AssignmentStmtCls::execute() " << endl;

    int rval = PExprCls(expr) -> evaluate();

    char *name = PIdentCls(ident) -> get_name();
    PSymtabCls scp = ScopeCls::get_vista();
    PSymtabEntryCls found_it = scp -> lookup(name);
    if (!found_it) {
        cout << "AsgmtStmt::execute() LOGIC ERROR" << endl;
        //should be done with an ErrorCls object
    } else {
        if (OptionCls::option_info() & 4) {
            if (rval > MAXINT) {
                cout << "Integer overflow" << endl;
                exit(1);
            }
        }
        PVarAttCls(found_it) -> set_value(rval);
    }
    return 0;
}
```

(e) Test that the -*C* option is actually detected by *ControllerCls*.

```
% epc -l f.p
[   1]    program example;
[   2]    begin
[   3]        i := 250;
[   4]        writeln(i)
[   5]    end.
       -> 250

% epc -l -C f.p
[   1]    program example;
[   2]    begin
[   3]        i := 250;
[   4]        writeln(i)
[   5]    end.
Integer overflow
%
```

B.6   Chapter 6 Activities

1. (a) Write C++ code defining, implementing and testing your own version of *ScanparseCls*.

```
class ScanparseCls {
    public:
        ScanparseCls();
    private:
};

#include <iostream.h>
#include "scanparse.h"

ScanparseCls :: ScanparseCls() {
    cout << "ScanparseCls()" << endl;
}

main() {
    ScanparseCls *scnprs = new ScanparseCls;
}
```

2. Construct a simple scanner for your project. You may find the following steps helpful.

   (a) Create a very simple parser specification file.

```
%token IDENTTK
%token INTEGERTK
%start program
%%
program: IDENTTK INTEGERTK
    ;
```

   (b) Create the corresponding set *y.tab.h* of token definitions.

```
yacc -d parser.gram
```

   (c) Create a scanner specification file.

```
digit    [0-9]
digits   {digit}+
letter   [A-Za-z]
ident    {letter}({letter}|{digit})*
whtspc   [ \t\n]
other    .
%%
{whtspc} {;}
{digits} {printf("found an integer\n");}
{ident}  {printf("found an identifier\n");}
{other}  {printf("other\n");}
%%
yywrap() {
    return 1;
}

main() {
    while (yylex()) {;}
}
```

(d) Build and test the scanner.

```
% lex scanner.specs
% cc lex.yy.c
% a.out
1222
found an integer
1 2 3
found an integer
found an integer
found an integer
1234a
found an integer
found an identifier
a1234
found an identifier
@
other
<ctrl D>
%
```

(e) Separately Compile and link your program with the C compiler:

> Nothing new in this exercise, except practice with the -c option
> and doing a separate linking, as described.

(f) Let's see what happens when we use C++ instead of C.

i. Compile lex.yy.c using the command CC -c lex.yy.c.

```
% CC -c lex.yy.c
CC  lex.yy.c:
"lex.yy.c", line 31: error:  undefined function yylook called
"lex.yy.c", line 34: error:  undefined function yywrap called
"lex.yy.c", line 29: warning: label yyfussy  not used
"lex.yy.c", line 289: error:  undefined function yyback called
"lex.yy.c", line 323: warning: old style definition of yyback()
"lex.yy.c", line 338: warning: old style definition of yyoutput()
"lex.yy.c", line 342: warning: old style definition of yyunput()
3 errors
%
```

ii. Note and correct the problems.

```
Insert the following code near the top of lex.yy.c.
int yylook();
int yywrap();
int yyback(int*,int);
Caution: these changes will disappear every time you use lex to generate
lex.yy.c.
```

iii. Test the new scanner.

```
% CC lex.yy.c
CC  lex.yy.c:
"lex.yy.c", line 32: warning: label yyfussy  not used
"lex.yy.c", line 326: warning: old style definition of yyback()
"lex.yy.c", line 341: warning: old style definition of yyoutput()
"lex.yy.c", line 344: warning: no value returned from yyoutput()
"lex.yy.c", line 345: warning: old style definition of yyunput()
"lex.yy.c", line 348: warning: no value returned from yyunput()
cc  -L/usr/local/lib   lex.yy.c -lC
% a.out
1 2 3 123 12a a12 +
found an integer
found an integer
found an integer
found an integer
found an integer
found an identifier
found an identifier
other
<ctrl D>
%
```

3. Construct a simple parser for your project. You may find the following steps helpful.

(a) Modify the parser specification file from Activity 2.

```
%token IDENTTK
%token INTEGERTK
%start program
%%
program: IDENTTK INTEGERTK
    ;
%%
void yyerror(char* msg) {
    printf("error -- %s\n");
}
```

And change the scanner so that it returns tokens to the parser.

```
%{
#include "y.tab.h"
%}

digit   [0-9]
digits  {digit}+
letter  [A-Za-z]
ident   {letter}({letter}|{digit})*
whtspc  [ \t\n]
other   .
%%
{whtspc} {;}
{digits} {return INTEGERTK;}
{ident}  {return IDENTTK;}
{other}  {;}
%%
yywrap() {
    return 1;
}
```

(b) Make a separate file containing *main()* and remove *main()* from the scanner specification file. This main just needs to make a single call to *yyparse()*.

```
extern int yyparse();
main() {
    yyparse();
}
```

(c) Separately compile the scanner, parser and main.

Place the function declarations back in *lex.yy.c*. Then add the following
similar ones to *y.tab.c* near the top.

```
#include <stdlib.h>
extern int yylex();
void yyerror(char*);
```

Compilation proceeds as follows.

```
% CC -c parser_mn.C
CC   parser_mn.C:
cc   -c  parser_mn.c
% CC -c lex.yy.c
CC  lex.yy.c:
"lex.yy.c", line 33: warning: label yyfussy  not used
"lex.yy.c", line 323: warning: old style definition of yyback()
"lex.yy.c", line 338: warning: old style definition of yyoutput()
"lex.yy.c", line 341: warning: no value returned from yyoutput()
"lex.yy.c", line 342: warning: old style definition of yyunput()
"lex.yy.c", line 345: warning: no value returned from yyunput()
cc   -c  lex.yy.c
% CC -c y.tab.c
CC  y.tab.c:
"parser1.specs", line 8: warning:  msg not used
"/usr/lib/yaccpar", line 85: warning:  statement not reached
"/usr/lib/yaccpar", line 64: warning:  yypvt used before set
"/usr/lib/yaccpar", line 442: warning: label yynewstate  not used
"/usr/lib/yaccpar", line 442: warning: label yyerrlab  not used
cc   -c  y.tab.c
%
```

Link the files and test the system.

```
% CC parser_mn.o lex.yy.o y.tab.o
cc  -L/usr/local/lib   parser_mn.o lex.yy.o y.tab.o -lC
% a.out
program 1
<ctrl D>
% a.out
1 program
error --
% a.out
1
error --
%
```

4. Include the simple scanner and parser from Activities 2 and 3 into the implementation module for *ScanparseCls*.

```
The definition can stay the same.

class ScanparseCls {
    public:
        ScanparseCls();
    private:
};
```

The implementation just includes *lex.yy.c* and *y.tab.c* and then makes a call to the parser.

```
#include <iostream.h>
#include "scanparse.h"

#include "lex.yy.c"
#include "y.tab.c"

ScanparseCls :: ScanparseCls() {
    cout << "ScanparseCls()" << endl;
    yyparse();
}

main() {
    ScanparseCls *scnprs = new ScanparseCls;
}
```

5. Now, let's flesh-out a "complete" scanparse module for your project.

The details of this should be fairly self explanatory. When you are completed you will probably have scanner and parser specification files which look much like those in the text. Perhaps your files will also include additional specifications of lexemes of productions based upon your own interests.

6. Extend your scanner specification file so that it also includes a regular expression that will recognize a valid Pascal real literal. Test your scanner on various correct and incorrect versions of real literals.

```
%{
#include "y.tab.h"
%}
digit    [0-9]
digits   {digit}+
dtdgts   {dot}{digits}
exponent [Ee]{sign}?{digits}
real     {digits}({dtdgts}|{exponent}|{dtdgts}{exponent})
whtspc   [ \t\n]
dot      "."
sign     [+\-]
other    .
%%
{whtspc} {;}
{digits} {printf("found an integer\n");}
{real}   {printf("found a real\n");}
{other}  {printf("found something else: %s\n",yytext);}
%%
yywrap() {
    return 1;
}
main() {
    while (yylex()) {;}
}
```

Test your scanner on various correct and incorrect versions of real literals.

```
% a.out
1.2
found a real
1.
found an integer
found something else: .
.3
found something else: .
found an integer
1e5
found a real
1E-5
found a real
1.E-5
found an integer
found something else: .
found something else: E
found something else: -
found an integer
1.0e+5
found a real
<ctrl D>
%
```

7. Extend your scanner specification file so that it includes a regular expression that recognizes a valid Pascal string literal.

```
%{
#include "y.tab.h"
%}

digit   [0-9]
digits  {digit}+
letter  [A-Za-z]
ident   {letter}({letter}|{digit})*
string  \'([^'\n]|\'\')+\'
whtspc  [ \t\n]
dot     "."
sign    [+\-]
other   .
%%
{whtspc} {;}
{digits} {printf("found an integer\n");}
{string} {printf("found a string\n");}
{ident}  {printf("found an ident\n");}
{other}  {printf("found something else: %s\n",yytext);}
%%
yywrap() {
    return 1;
}
main() {
    while (yylex()) {;}
}
```

Test your scanner on various correct and incorrect versions of string literals.

```
% a.out
'example string'
found a string
"bad string"
found something else: "
found an ident
found an ident
found something else: "
<ctrl D>
%
```

8. Extend your scanner/parser system to allow for the recognition of a selection statement.

(a) Add the required new tokens to the parser specification file.

```
%token EQTK NETK LTTK LETK GTTK GETK
```

(b) Modify your scanner specification file to return these new tokens.

Add the following scanner rules to return the relational operator tokens.

```
"=" {ckout(); return EQTK;}
"<>" {ckout(); return NETK;}
"<" {ckout(); return LTTK;}
"<=" {ckout(); return LETK;}
">" {ckout(); return GTTK;}
">=" {ckout(); return GETK;}
```

Modify the reserved word function..

```
rwtable_str rwtable[] = { //rw-tab
    "",             IDENTIFIERTK,
    "begin",        BEGINTK,
    "do",           DOTK,
    "else",         ELSETK,
    "end",          ENDTK,
    "for",          FORTK,
    "if",           IFTK,
    "program",      PROGRAMTK,
    "then",         THENTK,
    "to",           TOTK,
    "var",          VARTK,
    "writeln",      WRITETK
}; //end-rwtab
```

(c) Add the required productions to allow for the recognition of a selection statement.

```
IfStmt:
    IFTK Expr THENTK Statement
    ;
Expr:
    Factor
    | Factor RelOp Factor
    ;
RelOp:
    EQTK
    | NETK
    | LTTK
    | LETK
    | GTTK
    | GETK
    ;
Factor: /* as before ... */
```

(d) Test your expanded compiler on a source program that includes a selection statement that is valid for your syntax rule.

We'll test the system with a program like the following.

```
program example;
begin
    i := 250;
    if i < 300 then writeln(i);
    writeln(i);
    if (i < 500) then writeln(i);
end.
```

```
% epc -l f.p
[    1]     program example;
[    2]     begin
[    3]         i := 250;
[    4]         if i < 300 then writeln(i);
[    5]         writeln(i);
[    6]         if (i < 300) then writeln(i);
error has occurred...syntax error
%
```

9. Trace through the productions that are used to recognize the following program.

```
program trace;
begin
    i := 1;
    j := i;
    writeln(i);
end.
```

Using the line numbers to reference the productions on page 56, we have the following (left-most) derivation.

$$Program \overset{25}{\Rightarrow} \text{PROGRAMTK } Identifier \text{ SCTK } Block$$

$$\overset{65}{\Rightarrow} \text{PROGRAMTK IDENTIFIERTK SCTK } Block$$

$$\overset{30}{\Rightarrow} \text{PROGRAMTK IDENTIFIERTK SCTK}$$
$$\text{BEGINTK } StatementSeq \text{ ENDTK}$$

$$\overset{39}{\Rightarrow} \text{PROGRAMTK IDENTIFIERTK SCTK}$$
$$\text{BEGINTK}$$
$$StatementSeq \text{ SCTK } Statement$$
$$\text{ENDTK DOTTK}$$

$$\overset{39}{\Rightarrow} \text{PROGRAMTK IDENTIFIERTK SCTK}$$
$$\text{BEGINTK}$$
$$StatementSeq \text{ SCTK } Statement \text{ SCTK } Statement$$
$$\text{ENDTK DOTTK}$$

$$\overset{37}{\Rightarrow} \text{PROGRAMTK IDENTIFIERTK SCTK}$$
$$\text{BEGINTK}$$
$$Statement \text{ SCTK } Statement \text{ SCTK } Statement$$
$$\text{ENDTK DOTTK}$$

```
     ...     42     PROGRAMTK IDENTIFIERTK SCTK
             ⇒     BEGINTK
                   AssignmentStmt
                   SCTK Statement SCTK Statement
                   ENDTK DOTTK
             48     PROGRAMTK IDENTIFIERTK SCTK
             ⇒     BEGINTK
                   Identifier ASGTK Expr
                   SCTK Statement SCTK Statement
                   ENDTK DOTTK
             65     PROGRAMTK IDENTIFIERTK SCTK
             ⇒     BEGINTK
                   IDENTIFIERTK ASGTK Expr
                   SCTK Statement SCTK Statement
                   ENDTK DOTTK
             57     PROGRAMTK IDENTIFIERTK SCTK
             ⇒     BEGINTK
                   IDENTIFIERTK ASGTK Factor
                   SCTK Statement SCTK Statement
                   ENDTK DOTTK
             60     PROGRAMTK IDENTIFIERTK SCTK
             ⇒     BEGINTK
                   IDENTIFIERTK ASGTK Number
                   SCTK Statement SCTK Statement
                   ENDTK DOTTK
             65     PROGRAMTK IDENTIFIERTK SCTK
             ⇒     BEGINTK
                   IDENTIFIERTK ASGTK NUMLITERALTK
                   SCTK Statement SCTK Statement
                   ENDTK DOTTK
             45     PROGRAMTK IDENTIFIERTK SCTK
             ⇒     BEGINTK
                   IDENTIFIERTK ASGTK NUMLITERALTK
                   SCTK
                   AssignmentStmt
                   SCTK Statement
                   ENDTK DOTTK
             48     ...
             ⇒
```

B.7   Chapter 7 Activities

1. Write the implementation code for *SymtabEntryCls()* and *VarAttCls()*.

> It is quite instructive to construct a table using the structure illustrated in Figure 7.1. The main C++ syntax problem that must be solved is the assignment of a struct to a cell of your array.

2. Weinberger's algorithm is a very remarkable hashing function.

   (a) Describe this algorithm by carefully explaining:

   i. The loop in Line 58.

> Each character in the string s is used to produce the final hashing value. Characters are processed from left to right.

  ii. The shift and masking in Lines 59 and 60.

> Each character can be thought of as a 7- or 8-bit ASCII code. This integer is added to the previous hash value h after it has been shifted four bits. The last 4 bits of h will be those of the new character. Shifting the remaining bits and adding something to the last 3 or 4 bits certainly produces significantly different values of h even for strings differing only in the last digit.

 iii. The folding in Lines 61 and 62.

> Rather than loosing the top of h in the next shift, these values are bitwise XOR-ed with the previous result.

 iv. How the algorithm deals with strings of length greater than one.

> It is interesting to compare the algorithm's behavior on the three strings a, aa, and ab. The single character string produces to the ASCII value 141^1 (modulo the size of the table). If This value is shifted to the left four places it becomes 3020. When added to the next character the resulting values become 3161 or 3162, respectively. Even for a fairly small table size of, say 37, the corresponding hash values become 23, 21, and 22. Furthermore, it is also interesting that ac produces a collision with a hash value of 23. We often say that we want hash functions to map nearby strings to distant values. This excellent function does not do that.
>
> A little reflection indicates that, while some identifiers in a program are of the $i1$, $i2$ variety, most occur with much more random distances. What is probably more critical to the quality of function's performance is the distribution of hash values, given a more realistic sequence of input strings.

(b) i. Write a program that tests Weinberger's algorithm on each of the (upper- and lower-case) alphabetical characters. You may want to adjust the value of *tablesize*.

> The following code does a bit more. It uses words selected randomly from a system dictionary. Perhaps you might want to modify the rather trivial output. What is the mean number of entries? The median? A histogram of bucket sizes conveys much of the performance information. Aho et al. [2, page 436] describes a measure of the distribution and then indicates that this algorithm essentially meets the theoretical optimal value on a wide range of sample inputs.

```
#include <iostream.h>
#include <fstream.h>
#include <sys/time.h>
#include <libc.h>
#define NUMWRDS 125
#define NUMBUCKETS 71
#define MAXWRDSIZE 30
#define STATESIZE  64

int hash(char*);
int tablesize = NUMBUCKETS;               //a prime

main() {
    cout << "Testing Weinberger's algorithm" << endl;
    struct timeval tp;
    struct timezone tzp;
    char wrd[MAXWRDSIZE];
    int  bucket[NUMBUCKETS];
        for (int i= 0; i <= NUMBUCKETS; i++) {
            bucket[i] = 0;
        }
    char *infile = "/usr/dict/words";
    ifstream inFile(infile, ios::in);
    gettimeofday(&tp,&tzp);
    unsigned seed = (unsigned)(tp.tv_sec << 15);
    char state[STATESIZE];
    initstate(seed,state,STATESIZE);

    cout << "hashing " << hash("a") << " " << hash("aa") ;
    cout << " " << hash("ab")<< " " << hash("ac") << endl;
    for (int i_wrd = 0; i_wrd < NUMWRDS; i_wrd++) {
        char *w = wrd;
        long pos = (random() & 07777760000) >> 13;
        inFile.seekg(pos,ios::beg);
        char ch =' ';
        while (ch != '\n') {
            inFile.get(ch);
        }
        ch = ' ';
        for (int i_w= 0;
                    (i_w < MAXWRDSIZE)&&(ch != '\n');
                        i_w++) {
            inFile.get(ch);
            *w++ = ch;
        }
        *--w = '\0';
        cout << "dict word:  " << wrd ;
        cout << " hash value: " << hash(wrd) << endl;
        bucket[hash(wrd)]++;
    }
    for (int i_b = 0; i_b < NUMBUCKETS; i_b++) {
        cout << i_b << " " << bucket[i_b] << endl;
    }
}
```

ii. Test the algorithm an a larger selection of strings.

> The following are really not histograms: they're frequencies of frequencies. What we would really like to see is an exponential decay in the sizes of the boxes, i.e., the number of buckets that are hit should decrease as the number of hits increases. This doesn't happen in the first case, but this case doesn't reflect what happens in a symbol table since the table cannot contain more entries than the dimension of the array. The second case, even though also impossible shows just how good the algorithm really is. In this case there are still more entries than spaces but the characteristic decay is definitely occurring.

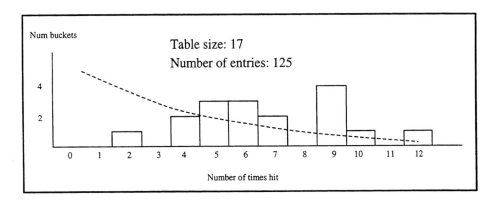

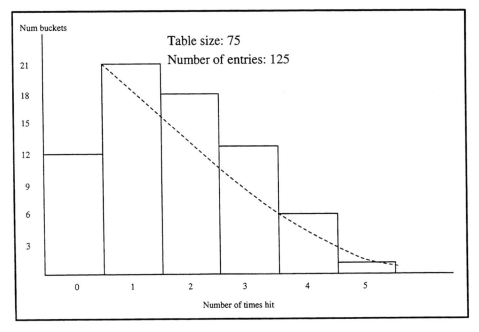

B.8   Chapter 8 Activities

1. Use a diagram something like Figures 8.1 and 8.2 to trace through the parse tree construction for the following program.

```
1   program Assigns;
2   begin
3       i := 1;
5       writeln(j);
4       j := i;
5       writeln(j)
6   end.
```

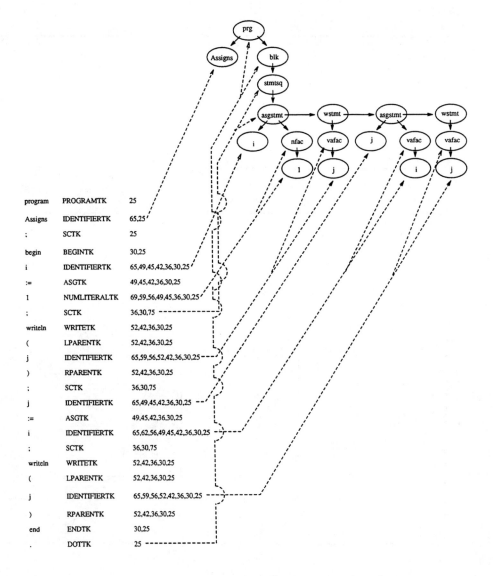

program	PROGRAMTK	25
Assigns	IDENTIFIERTK	65,25
;	SCTK	25
begin	BEGINTK	30,25
i	IDENTIFIERTK	65,49,45,42,36,30,25
:=	ASGTK	49,45,42,36,30,25
1	NUMLITERALTK	69,59,56,49,45,36,30,25
;	SCTK	36,30,75
writeln	WRITETK	52,42,36,30,25
(	LPARENTK	52,42,36,30,25
j	IDENTIFIERTK	65,59,56,52,42,36,30,25
)	RPARENTK	52,42,36,30,25
;	SCTK	36,30,75
j	IDENTIFIERTK	65,49,45,42,36,30,25
:=	ASGTK	49,45,42,36,30,25
i	IDENTIFIERTK	65,62,56,49,45,42,36,30,25
;	SCTK	36,30,75
writeln	WRITETK	52,42,36,30,25
(	LPARENTK	52,42,36,30,25
j	IDENTIFIERTK	65,59,56,52,42,36,30,25
)	RPARENTK	52,42,36,30,25
end	ENDTK	30,25
.	DOTTK	25

2. How would the example compiler behave with a program like the following?

```
1  program Assigns;
2  begin
3     i := 1;
4     j := i;
5     writeln(i,j)
6  end.
```

> The parse tree for the first two assignment statements would be built in essentially the same manner as Activity 1, above. An expression node would be built for the identifier *i*. Then at the comma, the parser would not be able to find a corresponding production and would print out an error message.

3. Define your own version of the *p_tree* module.

> The sample code in Appendix A should serve primarily as a starting point for your own definitions.

B.9 Chapter 9 Activities

1. Test your *p_tree* module by writing sample Pascal programs that will exercise each production in your grammar. You can test at least the order of creation of parse tree objects by 'turning on' the output messages at the beginning of each constructor.

> Start with a simple program like the following.
>
> ```
> program simple;
>     begin
>     end.
> ```
>
> This will test the highest level productions as will as that of the identifier leaf node. Also, be sure to verify that the statement sequence class is being created.
>
> Adding an assignment statement seems to be the next way to go. This will enable you to test expressions. Check that various *evaluate()* functions are returning correct values.
>
> Including an output statement or even an empty statement should most of the remaining productions.

2. *LstSeqBldrCls* is used not only for representing sequences of statements in a parse tree but also for a number of other very important list structures. One such application is the construction of the list of identifiers that may be used in a Pascal variable declaration.

(a) Modify your grammar to be able to recognize a list of identifiers that are separated by commas.

```
Ident_lst:
    Identifier
        {$$ = new IdentLstCls($1);}
    | Ident_lst COMMATK Identifier;
        {$$ = PIdentLstCls($1) -> append($3);}
    ;
Identifier:
    IDENTIFIERTK
        {$$ = new IdentCls();}
    ;
```

(b) Define and implement an *IdentLstCls* parse tree class.

```
typedef class IdentLstCls *PIdentLstCls;
class IdentLstCls : public PTreeNodeCls {
    public:
        IdentLstCls(PPTreeNodeCls Ident);
        PPTreeNodeCls append(PPTreeNodeCls);
        PIdentCls          get_seq_head()
                                {return seq_head;}
        PIdentCls          get_seq_tail()
                                {return seq_tail;}
    private:
        PIdentCls          seq_head;
        PIdentCls          seq_tail;
};
```

```
IdentLstCls :: IdentLstCls(PPTreeNodeCls Ident) {
    //cout << "IdentLstCls" << endl;
    seq_tail = seq_head = PIdentCls(Ident);
}

PPTreeNodeCls IdentLstCls :: append(PPTreeNodeCls Ident) {
    //cout << "IdentLstCls::append()" << endl;
    if (!seq_tail) {
        cerr << "IdentLstCls::append() -- LOGIC ERROR" << endl;
    } else {
        seq_tail = PIdentCls(seq_tail ->
                        LstSeqBldrCls::append(PIdentCls(Ident)));
    }
    return this;
}
```

(c) Modify the definition of *IdentCls* to allow for a **list** of *IdentCls* objects.

```
typedef class IdentCls  *PIdentCls;
class IdentCls : public PTreeNodeCls, public LstSeqBldrCls {
   public:
        IdentCls();
        char                *get_name();
};
```

3. In Activity 8 of Chapter 6 you extended the grammar to include some selection
   statement. Define and implement the corresponding parse tree classes.

```
typedef class IfStmtCls  *PIfStmtCls;
class IfStmtCls : public StatementCls {
   public:
        IfStmtCls()     {;}
        IfStmtCls(PPTreeNodeCls Expr,
                    PPTreeNodeCls Stmt1,
                        PPTreeNodeCls Stmt2);
        int             execute();
        int             emit();
   private:
        PPTreeNodeCls expr;
        PPTreeNodeCls stmt1;
        PPTreeNodeCls stmt2;
};
```

```
IfStmtCls :: IfStmtCls(PPTreeNodeCls Expr,
                       PPTreeNodeCls Stmt1,
                       PPTreeNodeCls Stmt2) {
    //cout << "IfStmtCls()" << endl;

    expr = Expr;
    stmt1 = Stmt1;
    stmt2 = Stmt2;
}
int IfStmtCls :: execute() {
    //cout << "IfStmtCls::execute()" << endl;
    if (PExprCls(expr) -> evaluate()) {
        PStatementCls(stmt1) -> execute();
    } else if (stmt2){
        PStatementCls(stmt2) -> execute();
    }
    return 0;
}
```

4. *NumLiteralCls* allows only for integer-valued numerical literals.

   (a) Define two subclasses, *IntLiteralCls* and *RealLiteralCls* which could be
       used to represent the two different types of numerical literals in the parse
       tree.

   > This extension is a bit more involved than it appears at first glance. The
   > first step is to modify the typing of *value* on *ExprCls*. Since this value
   > will need to store both integers and reals, it probably should be a string.
   > Moreover, *ExprCls* should also have a member indicating the type of
   > the expression. Subsequent operations on the value will then require
   > a translation of the string value to the appropriate literal value. The
   >
   > next step is to modify the scanner so that it can recognize the real and
   > integer literals and return appropriate tokens. Next, the grammar will
   >
   > need to be changed so that each of these new tokens will be examples
   > of a general numeric literal. The class definitions (initially can) contain
   >
   > only a constructor, since the value and type can be stored in the parent
   > *ExprCls*.

   (b) Implement *IntLiteralCls* and *RealLiteralCls*, being careful to impose some
       elementary semantic restriction on the values of each of the two types of
       literals.

   > Integer values should be checked against a standard maximum value.
   > Real values need to worry about both under and overflow.

(c) Incorporate these new classes into an extended compiler. Test your compiler on several source programs. Make special note of the kind of error messages that you might want to report in regard to this part of the compiler.

> Many of the details for this can be found in Holmes [5].

5. Explain why the constructor *IdentCls()* is able to access *PTreeNodeCls::lt*.

> The protected member *lt* of the base class behaves as a public member to a derived class (Lippman [5, page 182]).

6. As you read the implementation code for *ExprCls*, a nagging question begins to surface: Why all those recasting operators? In Line 86 of the implementation code for *NumFactorCls*, the argument *NumLit* is typed as a pointer to *PPTreeNodeCls* and later (Line 91) recast to a pointer to a NumLiteralCls. Why not just declare the argument to be of type *PNumLiteralCls* in the first place?

> There are essentially two approaches to the typing of the parser's value stack, $$. Traditional users of *yacc* have often typed the stack as a struct. In a "strongly"-typed environment, this requires constructing a union that anticipates at least all the major categories of parse tree nodes that are placed on that stack. In an object-oriented setting, the
>
> parser stack is declared to be of the parse tree node base class type. All objects placed on the stack are then accepted by the type-checker, since they are derived from the base class, by definition. However, when a *NumFactorCls* object is passed to a constructor by the parser, the C++ compiler has no way of determining its true class structure during the static semantic checking phase. Since we know (from the grammar) the exact nature of the object, we have to restore its true "type" by recasting.

7. List the way or ways in which the grammar influences the definition of the various classes of parse tree nodes. What kinds of changes to the grammar would induce changes to parse tree nodes?

> The grammar is the fundamental structure on which almost all the design details of the parse tree nodes depend.
>
> - There is almost a one-to-one correspondence between nonterminals and parse tree objects.
>
> - The number and type of nonterminals in the right side of each production determines the number and type of arguments for the corresponding class constructor. Often there will be a corresponding data member for each of these arguments, as well.
>
> - Class hierarchies depend on the grammar. If a nonterminal is on the left side of a number of productions, then any nonterminal representing any of the right sides will be a special case of the left side. (For example the various productions for Statement.) As such the class for any right nonterminal will then be derived from the class representing the left nonterminal.

8. We will extend the compiler by adding the following capabilities.

(a) Ability to handle source program comments.

> Add the following definition to the specification file for the scanner.
>
> ```
> comment ("{"[^}]*"}"|"(*"("*([^*])|[^*]")"|"*"[^)])*"*"*"*")")
> ```
>
> Then have the corresponding scanner action return nothing to the parser.

(b) Declaration of (integer) variables.

> The following steps seem to be a reasonable way to implement this extension.
>
> - Add the new tokens (eg., VARTK, ...).
> - Add the scanner rules for returning the new tokens.
> - Add the grammar productions for the declaration process.
> - Define and implement *IdentLstCls*. This extension was actually the content of Activity 2.
> - Define and implement *TypeSpecifierCls*.
> - Define and implement *VarDecCls*.
> - "Move" the symbol table code from the *IdentCls* constructor to *VarDecCls()*. Modify the symbol table code in *AssignmentStmtCls()* so that the use of an undeclared variable results in a warning.

```
Program:
    PROGRAMTK Identifier SCTK
    Var_dec_part
    Block
        {PProgramCls pgm = new ProgramCls($2,$5);}
    ;
Var_dec_part: /* empty */
    | VARTK Var_dec_lst SCTK
    ;
    Var_dec_lst: Var_dec
        | Var_dec_lst SCTK Var_dec
        ;
        Var_dec: Ident_lst COLONTK Type
            {$$ = new VarDecCls($1,$3);}
            ;
    Type:
        Identifier
            {$$ = new TypeSpecifierCls($1);}
        ;
```

```
typedef class TypeSpecifierCls *PTypeSpecifierCls;
class TypeSpecifierCls : public PTreeNodeCls {
    public:
        TypeSpecifierCls(PPTreeNodeCls);
};

typedef class VarDecCls *PVarDecCls;
class VarDecCls : public PTreeNodeCls {
    public:
        VarDecCls(PPTreeNodeCls IdentLst,
                        PPTreeNodeCls Type);
};
```

```
TypeSpecifierCls :: TypeSpecifierCls(PPTreeNodeCls Type) {
    //cout << "TypeSpecifierCls()" << endl;
    char *type_name = PIdentCls(Type) -> get_name();
    if (strcmp(type_name,"integer")) {
        cerr << "Variable type " << type_name ;
        cerr << " not supported" << endl;
    }
}


VarDecCls :: VarDecCls(PPTreeNodeCls IdentLst,
                       PPTreeNodeCls Type) {
    //cout << "VarDecCls()" << endl;
    if (!Type) {
        cerr << "VarDecCls: LOGIC ERROR" << endl;
    }
    PIdentCls id = PIdentLstCls(IdentLst)
                        -> get_seq_head();
    while (id) {
        char *name = id -> get_name();
        PSymtabCls scp = ScopeCls::get_vista();
        PSymtabEntryCls found_it = scp -> lookup(name);
        if (!found_it) {
            PVarAttCls va = new VarAttCls(name,0);
            scp -> insert(va);
        } else {
            cerr << "Redefinition of " << name << endl;
        }
    id = PIdentCls(id -> get_next());
    }
}
```

(c) Including an `if/else` statement.

The following (top-down!) steps are one way to attack the extension process.

- Add the required tokens.
- Add the productions for the *if* statement as well as the relational operations needed for Pascal boolean expressions.
- Define and implement *IfStmtCls*. Use normal object-oriented "stubbing" techniques to handle any references to classes not net defined. The *execute()* and *emit()* functions can also be roughed in.
- Add the *IfStmtCls* parser action to the grammar. Verify that and *IfStmtCls* is being placed on the parser's stack.
- Define and implement the six relational operators. Test the creation of the various operator objects.
- Implement the *execute()* and *emit()* member functions of *IfStmtCls*.

```
Expr:
    Factor
    | Factor RelOp Factor
        {$$ = PExprCls($2) -> add_children($1,$3);}
    ;
RelOp:
    EQTK
        {$$ = new EqCls;}
    | NETK
        {$$ = new NeCls;}
    | LTTK
        {$$ = new LtCls;}
    | LETK
        {$$ = new LeCls;}
    | GTTK
        {$$ = new GtCls;}
    | GETK
        {$$ = new GeCls;}
    ;
```

```
typedef class ExprCls  *PExprCls;
class ExprCls : public PTreeNodeCls {
   public:
        ExprCls();
        virtual int            evaluate();
        virtual int            emit();
        virtual PPTreeNodeCls  add_children(PPTreeNodeCls,
                                            PPTreeNodeCls);
   protected:
        int value;
};
typedef class EqCls *PEqCls;
class EqCls : public ExprCls{
    public:
        EqCls();
        int            evaluate();
        int            emit();
        PPTreeNodeCls  add_children(PPTreeNodeCls,
                                    PPTreeNodeCls);
    private:
        PPTreeNodeCls  left;
        PPTreeNodeCls  right;
};

typedef class NeCls *PNeCls;
class NeCls : public ExprCls{
    public:

    ...
```

```
PPTreeNodeCls ExprCls :: add_children(PPTreeNodeCls Left,
                              PPTreeNodeCls Right) {
    cout << "ExprCls::add_children()  BASE CLASS !!!!!!!" << endl;
    if (!(Left &&  Right)) {
        cerr << "ExprCls::add_children() LOGIC ERROR" << endl;
    }
    return 0;
}

EqCls :: EqCls() {
    //cout << "EqCls()" << endl;
}

int EqCls :: evaluate() {
    //cout << "EqCls::evaluate()" << endl;
    return (PExprCls(left)->evaluate() ==
                          PExprCls(right)->evaluate());
}

PPTreeNodeCls EqCls :: add_children(PPTreeNodeCls Left,
                              PPTreeNodeCls Right) {
    //cout << "EqCls::add_children()" << endl;
    left = Left;
    right = Right;
    return this;
}
```

B.10   Chapter 10 Activities

1. Describe or summarize in words the implementation details of the following classes.

- EmptyStmtCls

  The empty statement *execute()* is essentially a no-op, returning the integer value 0 that indicates a completed execution of the statement.[2]

- AssignmentStmtCls

  In the project's original form, assignment classes are responsible for entering any new identifiers into the symbol table. The expression on the right side of the assignment is evaluated. The symbol table entry containing the identifier on the left side is then updated with the value.

- WriteStmtCls

  WriteStmtCls::execute() simple outputs the value of the expression data membe

- StatementSeqCls

> The sequence of statements in the block has been represented by a linked list of statement objects. *StatementSeq::execute()* just requests that each of these statement objects execute itself.

- BlockCls

> *BlockCls::execute()* just asks its *stmt_seq* data member to execute itself.

- ProgramCls

> ProgramCls::execute() requests that its block data member execute itself.

- PTreeCls

> *PTreeCls* has its *root* data member pointing to the *ProgramCls* object. *PTreeCls::execute()* is therefore just requesting the root of the parse tree to begin interpreting the program.

2. Implement your own versions of the various *execute()* member functions.

3. Test your compiler on the empty, **writeln**, and assignment statements.

4. (a) Complete the implementation of the classes in Activity (8,6).

> Most of the details have already been given in the answers to Activities 9.3 and 9.8, above.

   (b) Test your compiler on boundary examples.

> There are a number of interesting boundary conditions. The implementation described in this chapter does not check to see that the selection expression is in fact a boolean expression. Test the program on a statement containing other forms of expressions. Can you think of other languages that behave this way?
>
> Trying to bullet-proof your compiler at this stage is probably not a wise use of time, unless your enhancement includes semantic analysis.

5. Write and test an interpreter that traverses the parse tree.

> This is really a major project in itself. If you wish to share your work, please feel free to contact me and I will try to make it available to other interested people.

B.11   Chapter 11 Activities

1. Implement your own versions of the various *emit()* functions.

2. Test your *emit()* functions:

3. This question requires access to SPARCstation documentation such as the SPARC Architecture Manual [11] or Paul's excellent new text [9].

(a) What is the purpose of the .align pseudo op?

> Our use of the data segment is primarily as a place to allocate storage space for the various program variables. In a more normal compiling situation, variables will require differing amounts of memory. Since the load and store instructions are among the most used in normal programming situations,[3] their data storage requirements become de facto standards for the placement of almost all program data.
>
> Integer load and store instructions support byte, halfword (16-bit), word (32-bit), and doubleword (64-bit) accesses. Half-words must be aligned on 2-byte boundaries, word accesses on 4-byte boundaries, and doubleword on 8-byte boundaries. The align 2 pseudo-op ensures that the address where the next data will be assigned will be evenly divisible by 2, i.e., on a 2-byte boundary. The same kind of thing is true for align 4 and align 8.

(b) The *sethi* instruction is actually a hardware instruction that has been transcribed to software. Describe this instruction

> Machine instructions occupy a single 32-bit word. Of these bits, 8 are reserved to represent the instruction, 15 are used for 3 5-bit representations of the various registers being referenced. This leaves only 9 instruction bits, one of which indicates whether or not the second register is being used. If the second register is not being used, then there are a maximum of 13 bits that can be used for a signed immediate constant. That's not a very big number.
>
> If we want to load or store a 32-bit integer we use the sethi instruction that loads the high 22 bits of a register, clearing the low 10 bits. The low bits of the integer can then moved using an or command.

(c) Describe the unary operators %*lo* and %*hi*.

> In order to use the sethi command, the value must be first shifted to the right 10 bits since the right-most bits are the ones accessed by sethi. The operator %$hi(x)$ makes this shift on the value x. Then the low 10 bits of the value must be or-ed with the new value. The operator %$lo(x)$ does this.

4. Modify the code generator module to produce code for another cpu.

> Again, this is really a major project. If you wish to share this work as well, please contact me and I will make it available to other interested people.

Bibliography

[1] R. Abbott. Program design by informal english descriptions. *Communications of the ACM*, 26(11), 1983.

[2] Alfred V. Aho, Ravi Sethi, and Jeffery D. Ullman. *Compilers, Principles, Techniques, and Tools.* Addison-Wesley, Reading, MA, 1986.

[3] Grady Booch. *Object Oriented Design with Applications.* Benjamin/Cummings, Redwood City, CA, 1991.

[4] Doug Cooper. *Condensed Pascal.* Norton, New York, 1987.

[5] Jim Holmes. *Object-Oriented Compiler Construction.* Prentice Hall, Englewood Cliffs, NJ, 1995.

[6] John E Hopcroft and Jeffrey D. Ullman. *Introduction to Automata theory, Languages, and Computation.* Addison-Wesley, Reading, MA, 1979.

[7] Ed Krol. *The Whole Internet User's Guide and Catalog.* O'Reilly & Associates, Sebastopol, CA, 1992.

[8] Stanley B. Lippman. *C++ Primer.* Addison-Wesley, Reading, MA, 1989.

[9] Richard P. Paul. *SPARC Architecture, Assembly language Programming Language and C.* Prentice Hall, Englewood Cliffs, NJ, 1994.

[10] Axel T. Schreiner and H. George Friedman, Jr. *Introduction to Compiler Construction with UNIX.* Prentice Hall, Englewood Cliffs, NJ, 1985.

[11] SPARC International, Inc. *The SPARC Architecture Manual.* Prentice Hall, Englewood Cliffs, NJ, 1992.

[12] Bjarne Stroustrup. *The C++ Programming Language.* Addison-Wesley, Reading, MA, 1987.

[13] Niklaus Wirth. The programming language pascal. *Acta Informatica*, 1(1):35–63, 1971.

Index

action
    parser, 77
arguments
    command line, 29
AssignmentStmtCls
    definition, 87
attributes, 65

base class, 81
binding
    late, 83
blastula, 16
BlockCls
    definition, 90
    implementation, 103, 109, 119

C++
    comment, 27
    include, 28
    input, 28
    output, 28
    pointers, 29
cerr, 29
cin, 28
ckout, 50
class, 3
    class body, 3
    class head, 3
class implementation, 5
code generation, 111
constructor, 3
ControllerCls
    definition, 34

implementation, 32, 36, 37
cout, 28
csect
    bss, 112
    data, 112
    text, 112

derived, 81
directives, 28

EmptyStmtCls
    definition, 87
endl, 28
epc program code, 123
essential subsystems, 17
executable
    producing, 119
ExprCls
    definition, 85
    implementation, 99, 116
extraction, 28

ftp, viii

IdentCls
    definition, 84
    implementation, 98
identifier, 65
implementation file
    class-oriented, 81
    function-oriented, 81
implementation guidelines, 17
inherit, 81

instance, 3
instantiate, 77
interpreter
    execute()
      return value, 108
    makefile, 109
involvement, vii

keyword, 3

late binding, 83
leaf class, 84
lexeme specification, 48
LexTokCls
    definition, 43
    implementation, 44
LstSeqBldrCls
    definition, 88
    implementation, 102

main()
    implementation, 27
make, 21
makefile, 21, 22
    ctrl, 38
    main, 29
    p_tree, 104
      emit, 120
      interp, 109
    scanparse, 59
    symtab, 72
manipulator, 28
milestones, 21
morula, 16
multiple inheritance, 89

NumFactorCls
    implementation, 100, 101
NumLiteralCls
    definition, 84
    implementation, 96

object, 3
OptionCls
    definition, 33

implementation, 33

p_tree makefile, 104
parser
    header, 54
    productions, 56
    sed commands, 58
    tokens, 45, 55
    user-supplied functions, 58
parser action, 77
parser value stack, 77
preprocessor, 28
private, 3
ProgramCls
    definition, 90
    implementation, 103, 109, 119
PTreeCls
    definition, 91
    implementation, 104, 118
PTreeNodeCls
    definition, 83
    implementation, 96
public, 3

reduced production, 77
regular expressions, 48
relationship
    subclass, 34
    uses, 35
reserved words
    checking for, 51
    table, 51

SampleCls
    definition, 3
scanner
    actions, 48
    rules, 48
    sed commands, 53
ScanParseCls
    definition, 45
    implementation, 43–45
scope, 65, 73
ScopeCls

definition, 66
segment, 112
    bss, 112
    data, 112
    text, 112
standard output, 28
StatementCls
    definition, 86
    implementation, 101, 107, 117
StatementSeqCls
    definition, 89
    implementation, 102, 108, 118
string editor: sed, 52
StringCls, 8, 148
SymtabCls
    definition, 67
    implementation, 70–72, 115
SymtabEntryCls
    definition, 67
    implementation, 115
system directory structure, 19
system functions, 120
system modules, 17

tag name, 3
token
    definition, 47

value stack, 77
virtual member, 83
vista, 66, 73

writeln.o, 120
WriteStmtCls
    definition, 87

YYSTYPE, 54

DATE DUE